KU-561-393

Mongolian
PHRASEBOOK & DICTIONARY

Acknowledgments
Associate Publisher Mina Patria
Associate Product Director Angela Tinson
Product Editor Elizabeth Jones
Series Designer James Hardy
Language Writer Alan JK Sanders, J Bat-Ireedui, Tsogt Gombosuren
Cover Image Researcher Naomi Parker

Thanks
Larissa Frost, Carol Jackson, Michael Kohn, Chris Love,
Wayne Murphy, Branislava Vladisavljevic

Published by Lonely Planet Publications Pty Ltd
ABN 36 005 607 983

3rd Edition – March 2014
ISBN 978 1 74321 184 7
Text © Lonely Planet 2014
Cover Image Woman talking to a Buddhist monk, Gandan Khiid
monastery, Ulaanbaataar, Mongolia, Jorge Fernandez / Alamy ©
Printed in China 10 9 8 7 6 5 4 3 2

Contact lonelyplanet.com/contact

All rights reserved. No part of this publication may be reproduced, stored in a retrieval system or
transmitted in any form by any means, electronic, mechanical, photocopying, recording or otherwise,
except brief extracts for the purpose of review, without the written permission of the publisher.
Lonely Planet and the Lonely Planet logo are trade marks of Lonely Planet and are registered
in the U.S. Patent and Trademark Office and in other countries. Lonely Planet does not allow its
name or logo to be appropriated by commercial establishments, such as retailers, restaurants
or hotels. Please let us know of any misuses: www.lonelyplanet.com/ip

Although the authors and Lonely Planet try to make the information
as accurate as possible, we accept no responsibility for any loss, injury
or inconvenience sustained by anyone using this book.

Paper in this book is certified against the Forest Stewardship Council™
standards. FSC™ promotes environmentally responsible, socially
beneficial and economically viable management of the world's forests.

MIX
Paper from
responsible sources
FSC™ C021741
www.fsc.org

Contents

Introduction

Mongolian, or Mongol as it is also referred to, is an Altaic language, distantly related to Turkish as well as Turkic languages of Central Asia like Kazakh and Tuvan, and displays their typical features of agglutination and vowel harmony. While these features are unfamiliar to speakers of English and most other European languages, they need not present difficulties once the basic principles have been grasped. Briefly, agglutination means that word stems are invariable and inflection (tense, case, etc) is achieved by the addition to the word stems of single or multiple suffixes. Vowel harmony means that all the vowels in a word stem, and any suffixes attached to it, belong to one class of either 'back' or 'front' vowels, which are not mixed. These features are explained with examples in the Grammar and Pronunciation chapters respectively.

There are about seven million Mongol speakers in the world, including two million in independent Mongolia (the former Mongolian People's Republic), more than twice that number in Inner Mongolia and other parts of China, and another half million or so in the Buryat and Kalmyk Republics and elsewhere in Russia. Khalkh Mongol, named after Mongolia's largest ethnic group and the country's official language, is also spoken in parts of Inner Mongolia and China's north-eastern provinces. Mongols living elsewhere in China and Russia and small related groups in Mongolia itself such as Oirats and Buryats speak forms of Mongol which are somewhat different from Khalkh.

The basic Mongol-Turkic vocabulary of Khalkh, which was centred on the nomadic way of life, has been subjected to a wide range of influences since the time of the Mongol Empire.

5

Buddhism brought with it religious terminology in Tibetan and Sanskrit, and Manchu and Chinese words and titles were added during the Qing dynasty. Russian technical terms and political phraseology were introduced during communist rule this century. Nowadays English is the most popular foreign language in Mongolia and Mongolised English words ranging from 'broker' to 'hobby' have entered circulation.

The Mongols have written their language in several different scripts, the oldest and most durable of which, called the classical Mongol script, was introduced almost 800 years ago under Genghis Khan. Derived from Uighur writing, it has 24 letters written vertically in initial, medial and final variants. The language of the classical Mongol script is now archaic, Khalkh having undergone many changes over the centuries.

Although the classical script is still used by Mongols living in Inner Mongolia and elsewhere in China, its use in Mongolia was discouraged following the introduction of a modified Cyrillic (Russian) alphabet in the 1940s. Mongolia's democratic revolution in the early 1990s led to demands for the restoration of the classical script. However, its planned official reintroduction in 1994, initially for government publications, was postponed until the turn of the century because of the lack of proper preparation, shortage of publishing facilities, and also resistance from the many Mongols who wanted to stick to Cyrillic.

You will find plenty of opportunities to use this phrasebook in Mongolia, even though there are lots of 'biznesmen' and students in Ulan Bator eager to practise their English. Outside the city centre, and especially in the countryside, you will want to communicate with people who speak only Mongol. If no one understands what you're reading from the book, just point to the Mongol Cyrillic on the right hand side.

This phrasebook is intended to accompany Lonely Planet's *Mongolia - a travel survival kit*. Used together these books will make your Mongolian travels a lot easier.

Getting Started

Before reading any further, you might like to memorise a few of the most essential words you'll be using (and hearing) in your travels. If you don't have time to learn more than these, at least you'll have enough to make your stay more rewarding.

'Hello' is *sain bainuu* (the **ai** is pronounced as 'eye'), and the appropriate response is *sain ta sain bainuu*. See pages 32 to 34 for more greetings. There is no particular word for 'please' and several ways to say 'thank you' (see page 35), but you won't be wrong saying *bayarlaa* ('thanks').

'How much is it?' is *en yamar üntei ve?* (see page 26 for how to make questions). 'Yes' is *tiim* and 'No' is *ügüi*, although when you get more confident, you can just repeat the verb — see page 28.

'I don't understand' is *bioilgokhgüi bain*. For more on communication and language difficulties, try page 51.

Good luck and *sain yavaarai!* ('safe journey!').

Pronunciation

Khalkh Mongol, the national language of Mongolia, is spoken without appreciable regional variation almost everywhere except a few parts of the country's westernmost provinces. The sounds are not specially difficult to pronounce, and with practice you will get used to stressing long vowels and following the rules of vowel harmony outlined below. With practice you will also gradually find it easier to understand what people are saying to you. When you ask questions, encourage people to answer slowly and to repeat the answer if necessary. They will be pleased and amused that you are taking the trouble to learn their language.

Script

The 35 letters of the Mongolian Cyrillic script are those of the Russian alphabet plus two additional ones (ө and ү) to represent 'ö' and 'ü'. Some letters of the Russian alphabet are pronounced differently in Mongol, however, and some others are used only to write words which have entered Mongol from Russian.

In this book the letters of the Mongolian Cyrillic alphabet have been given the following English written equivalents (transliteration). Because Mongolian Cyrillic has more letters than the English alphabet, some Cyrillic letters are represented by two or more English letters.

Аа	a	Бб	b	Вв	v
Гг	g	Дд	d	Ее	ye
Ёё	yo	Жж	j	Зз	z
Ии	i	Йй	i	Кк	k
Лл	l	Мм	m	Нн	n
Оо	o	Өө	ö	Пп	p
Рр	r	Сс	s	Тт	t
Уу	u	Үү	ü	Фф	f
Хх	kh	Цц	ts	Чч	ch
Шш	sh	Щщ	shch	Ъъ	(no sound)
Ыы	y	Ьь	i	Ээ	e
Юю	yu	Яя	ya		

Transliteration schemes like this are used for example for writing Mongolian personal and place-names in English. In other English publications you may come across variations like *dzh* for 'j' (ж), *dz* for 'z' (з), *h* for 'kh' (х) and ' (single quote) for 'short' 'i' (ь), as well as the use of additional diacritical marks (accents). The letter ъ, written between some consonants and vowels to alter the quality of the consonants, may be ignored. There is no agreed international system of transliteration. A map of China and Mongolia on sale in English-speaking countries but published in Germany, for example, uses yet another scheme with *c* for ts (ц), *j* for i (й), *ja* for ya (я), *ž* for j (ж), *š* for sh (ш), etc.

The Mongol Cyrillic script is not phonetic and transliteration alone, whichever scheme is used, can give only a rough indication of pronunciation. Some words have no standard spelling, some letters are not always pronounced, others are pronounced in a different order from that written. The guide to pronunciation used in this book takes account of this.

Consonants

Most of the consonants are pronounced as they would be in English, but the following combinations should be noted:

ч	**ch**	as the 'ch' in 'chat'
ж	**j**	as the 'j' in 'jewel'
х	**kh**	as the 'ch' in 'loch'
ш	**sh**	as the 'sh' in 'shoe'
щ	**shch**	as the 'shch' in 'cash-cheque'
ц	**ts**	as the 'ts' in 'cats'
з	**z**	as the 'ds' in 'fads'

The letter *g* (г), when at the end of a word (final), sounds between *g* and 'k'. The letter *v* (в), when final, is between *v* and *w*, and a final *n* may sound like *ng*. The combination *sch* is not one but two letters, *s* + *ch* (сч) pronounced like the *sch* in ek-schange' (exchange). Most Mongols do not distinguish between *p* and *f* or between *kh* and *k* (*f* and *k* are found only in loan words). They also find words beginning with *r* difficult to pronounce without an initial vowel: *oros* (орос, Russian), *oryoong* (район, region), etc.

Vowels

Mongolian vowels are short or long. The short vowels are:

а	**a**	as the 'u' in 'but'
э	**e**	as the 'e' in 'den'
и	**i**	as the 'i' in 'tin'
о	**o**	as the 'o' in the British 'hot'

ө	**ö**	as the 'o' in 'money'
у	**u**	as the 'ou' in 'source'
ʏ	**ü**	as the 'o' in 'who'

Long vowels are doubled short vowels:

аа	**aa**	as the 'a' in 'bar'
ээ	**ee**	as the 'ei' in 'deign'
ий	**ii**	as the 'ee' in 'teem'
оо	**oo**	as the 'o' in 'horn'
өө	**öö**	as the 'e' in 'fern'
уу	**uu**	as the 'o' in 'bone'
ʏʏ	**üü**	as the 'oo' in 'soon'

The single vowel 'y' is also long:

| ы | **y** | as the 'i' in 'ill' |

It is important to emphasise long vowels since the length differentiates meaning, eg *tsas/tsaas* (snow/paper), *üd/üüd* (noon/door).

Some vowels can start with a y-sound (long form in brackets):

я	**ya**	as the 'ya' in 'yard' (*yaa*/яа)
е	**ye**	as the 'ye' in 'yes'
ё	**yo**	as the 'ya' in 'yacht' (*yoo*/ёо)
е	**yö**	as the 'yea' in 'yearn'
ю	**yu**	as the 'yo' in 'yoyo' (*yuu*/юу)
ю	**yü**	as the 'you' in 'you' (*yüü*/юу)

Vowels may combine to form diphthongs:

ай	**ai**	as the 'eye' in 'eyes'
эй	**ei**	as the 'ay' in 'pay'
иа	**ia**	as the 'ia' in 'Fiat'
ио	**io**	as the 'io' in 'senior'
иу	**iu**	as the 'u' in 'union'
ой	**oi**	as the 'oy' in 'boy'
уа	**ua**	as the 'wo' in 'wonder'
уай	**uai**	as the 'wi' in 'wine'
уй	**ui**	as the 'we' in 'week'
үй	**üi**	as the 'oui' in 'Louis'

Words ending in the letter ь are written in the pronunciation guide with a short unstressed *i* after a short or long stressed vowel, eg *ail* (аль) 'which', *goiv* (говь) 'Gobi' and *surguuil* (сургууль) 'school'.

Vowel Harmony

Vowels are classed as 'back' or 'front' and are 'harmonised', that is to say, different classes cannot be mixed within the same word:

- 'back' vowels are *a, o, u, y* (and *ya, yo, yu*), as in *zurgaa* (six), *nomyn* (book's), *yamar* (what), *yostoi* (must), etc.
- 'front' vowels are *e, ö, ü* (and *ye, yö, yü*), also initial *i*, as in *önöödör* (today), *yösdügeer* (ninth), *irvüü* (did come?), etc.

Otherwise *i* is neutral and can be mixed with back or front vowels, eg *ajil* (work), *öchigdör* (yesterday).

The vowels of suffixes match those of the stem to which they are attached, producing a wide range of variations in pronunciation and spelling. The noun suffix 'long vowel plus -r' ('by means of'), for example, -*aar* as in *ag**aa**raar,* meaning 'by air (mail)', has the following variants:

-*eer*, -*oor* and -*öör* according to the stem vowels after consonants:

delg**üür**-*eer*	round the shops
mongol-*oor*	in Mongolian
ödr-**öör**	by day

-*gaar*, -*geer*, -*goor* and -*güür* after long vowels:

sh**uu**dang-*aar*	via the post office
tolg**oi**-*goor*	with the head
ögl**öö**-*güür*	in the morning

-*iar* and -*ior* for stems ending in *i,* eg:

mor-**ior**	on horseback

Similarly, the verbal suffix -*val* ('if ...', which is the same for all persons and numbers) has the variants -*vel*, -*vol*, -*völ* according to the vowels of the verb stem, as well as -*bal*, -*bel*, -*bol* and -*böl* after stems ending in -*l*, -*m* or -*v*, including the following combinations:

ir + *vel*	**i**r*vel*	if (you) come
or + *vol*	**o**r*vol*	if (they) leave
yav + *bal*	*ya***v**b*al*	if (I) go, etc.

PRONUNCIATION

The negative suffix *-güi* can be attached to back or front stems: *baikhgüi* (there isn't any), *ireegüi* (didn't come), etc.The Mongolian personal or place names which seem to break the rules of vowel harmony, eg *Sükhbaatar, Luvsanchültem, Öndörkhaan* etc, although written as one word consist of two (or more) separate words.

Stress & Emphasis

Stressed vowels are printed in bold type. In words with short vowels the stress is on the first short vowel: eg *olon* (many). Any other short vowels are reduced and become indistinct (such a vowel is known as a 'schwa'; an example in English would be the 'e' in 'open').

In words with one long vowel or diphthong the stress is on the long vowel (or diphthong): eg *ulaan* (red), *dalai* (sea). Under the influence of a long vowel a short vowel is reduced or may disappear: *olon* (many), *olnoo* (by many).

In words with more than one long vowel the regular stress is on the penultimate long vowel: eg *gantsaaraa* (on one's own), *ööriigöö* (oneself), *uuchlaarai!* (sorry!).

Note that the parts of multiple personal and place names are stressed separately: *Gombosüren, Bayan-Ölgii, Ulaanbaatar*.

The interrogative particles *uu* (*üü*) and *ve* (*be*) and affirmative particle *bii* at the end of a sentence are stressed: *sain bainuu?* (How are you?); *ter khaan bain ve?* (Where is he?); *chamd en nom bii yuu?* (Do you have this book?); *nadad bii* (I have).

The speaker's own emphasis at the end of a sentence can lengthen a final vowel and/or shift the stress: *tanaikhan gertee oluulaa suudaguu?* (Do you have a large family? lit: Are there many of you living at home?), *manaikhan oluulaa!* (We certainly do have a large family! lit: There are many of us!). Similarly, *sain bainaa!* (I'm fine!), *bolnoo!* (Certainly you may!) and *uuchlaarai!* (Sorry!).

PRONUNCIATION

Grammar

This chapter presents the basics of Mongolian grammar, so you can get an idea of how sentences are put together. Maybe even put together your own (let's be ambitious)! Before plunging into the details, it might be useful to check some of the terms used. Of course, you can just skip this section if you are already familiar with them.

Grammatical Terms

The base of a Mongolian word is called the stem. The attachments to the end of a stem are called suffixes. The suffixes are of two kinds. Derivational suffixes form new words from existing stems, that is, deriving new meanings. Inflectional suffixes inflect words, that is, changing them to express tense, gender, number, case, etc (see the following section on Word Formation).

Inflectional suffixes include case suffixes, which inflect nouns, pronouns, etc, and tense suffixes, which inflect verbs. The case is the way words in a sentence relate to one another; sometimes this is controlled by particular prepositions.

Mongolian has seven grammatical cases:

• nominative — indicating the subject (actor) of a verb
• accusative —indicating the direct object (recipient)of an action
• genitive — indicating possession
• dative/locative — indicating an indirect object, or place, or time

16

• instrumental — indicating a means or instrument
• ablative — indicating movement away
• comitative — indicating togetherness

There is also a simple vocative, used when calling people by name or title. Each case has its own distinctive set of suffixes (see the section on Case Suffixes, page 19).

Grammatical number is singular or plural. Grammatical person is the speaker (first person, in English 'I, we'), the person spoken to (second person, 'you'), or the person spoken of (third person, 'he, she, it, they').

The tenses of the verb indicate the time or completion of an action, etc, and include the present/future, past and perfective. Mongolian has a wide range of suffixes for verb forms which have no exact parallels in English. Some of the more useful ones are explained in this chapter.

GRAMMAR

Word Formation

Mongolian words consist of invariable stems and variable suffixes which may be attached to them. The stems are carriers of basic meaning, eg the noun *ger* meaning a 'yurt' or 'felt tent', and also 'home'. The suffixes have no meaning of their own and cannot occur alone, but they modify the meaning of the stems. Derivational suffixes create new stems, eg from the noun *ger* the verb *ger-lekh* meaning 'to get married' (ie acquire one's own yurt), and *ger-lüü-lekh* , 'to marry off'.

Inflectional suffixes play the role of noun declension, eg *ger-iin* meaning 'of a yurt' (lit: 'yurt-of'), or verb conjugation, eg *ger-lee* meaning 'married' (lit: 'yurt-has acquired'). The vowels in a suffix match those of the stem to which it is attached. This typical feature of Mongolian and other Altaic languages is called vowel harmony (see the Pronunciation chapter, page 12).

Sentence & Word Order

The Mongolian word order is subject-object-verb. 'I am studying Mongolian' follows the order 'I (subject) Mongol-language
(object) studying (verb)':

I am studying Mongolian.   *bi mongol khel üzej bain*

Adjectives stand before the noun(s) they describe:

big	*ikh*
big shop (department store)	*ikh delgüür*

Adjectives follow any other noun in the possessive case (see Case
Suffixes below):

food shop	*khünsnii delgüür* (lit: food-of shop)
supermarket	*khünsnii ikh delgüür* (lit: food-of big shop)

Nouns

The noun stem is the base form to which inflectional suffixes are
attached. Dictionaries of Mongolian list nouns as stems, without
suffixes. Mongolian nouns have no grammatical gender, that is,
no masculine/feminine/neuter forms, and there is no definite or
indefinite article:

(the/a) waiter/waitress   *üilchlegch*

Nouns which are one word in English may be pairs in Mongolian:

hotel	*zochid buudal* (lit: visitors' dismounting-place)
banknote	*möngön temdegt* (lit: silver seal-with)
tableware	*ayag khalbag* (lit: glass and spoon)

GRAMMAR

Plurals

The plural is used much less often in Mongolian than in English. The singular form of the noun is sufficient when the quantity is unspecified or specified by a numeral:

books	*nom**uud***
three books	*gu**rvan nom*
I'd like to buy some books.	*bi nom avmaar bain*

Noun plurals are formed by the suffixes *-d* or *-uud*, but some nouns describing people are made plural by the postposition *nar*:

visitor	*zochin*
visitors	*zochid*
book	*nom*
books	*nom**uud***
lama (Buddhist priest)	*lam*
lamas	*lam nar*
teacher	*bagsh*
teachers	*bagsh nar*

GRAMMAR

Case Suffixes

When a particular thing is specified, the objective (accusative) suffix *-g* is added to the noun stem with appropriate linking vowels (see Vowel Harmony in the Pronunciation chapter, page 12):

I'd like to buy this book.	*bi en nom-**yg** avmaar bain*
	(lit: I this book-*yg* like to buy am)
I'd like to buy these books.	*bi en nom**uud**-yg avmaar bain*
	(lit: I this books-*yg* like to buy am)
He took the horse.	*mor-**iig** a**vav***
	(lit: horse-*iig* [he] took)

To show possession, the noun suffix for the genitive case is based on -*n* with appropriate linking vowels:

state (state's) department store	*uls-yn ikh delgüür*
	(lit: state-*yn* big shop)
human rights	*khün-ii erkh*
	(lit: man-*ii* right)
post office box	*shuudang-iin khairtsag*
	(lit: post-*iin* box)

To indicate a place or time, the noun suffix for the dative-locative case is based on -*d* or -*t* :

in the water	*usan-d*
in the hand	*gar-t*
when I was small	*minii bag-ad*

To show how something is done, the noun suffix for the instrumental case is based on a long vowel plus -*r* :

by air (mail)	*agaar-aar*
on horseback	*mor-ior*
during the night	*shön-öör*

To show where something comes from, the noun suffix for the ablative case is based on a long vowel plus -*s* :

from (the) town	*khot-oos*
from the younger brother	*düü-gees*
because (lit: from the reason)	*uchr-aas*

To mean 'together with' something, the noun suffix for the comitative case is based on -*tai, -toi* etc:

GRAMMAR

with (having) a horse	*mor-toi*
sunny (lit: with sun)	*nar-tai*
famous (lit: with name)	*ner-tei*

Pronouns

There are personal pronouns in Mongol for the first ('I, we') and second ('you') persons but not the third — the demonstrative pronouns 'this' and 'that' are used for 'he', 'she' and 'it' without gender distinction:

I	*bi*	we	*bid*
you (inf)	*chi*	you (pl)	*ta nar*
you (sg)	*ta*		
he/she/it/that	*ter*	they/those	*ted nar*
this	*en*	these	*ed nar*

To distinguish between 'he' and 'it', you can say *ter khün* (that person) or *ter yum* (that thing), etc. The informal 'you' *chi* is used for children and amongst close relatives and friends.

Note some of the other case forms of the pronouns: eg *nadad*, 'to me'; *bidend*, 'to us'; *tantai*, 'with you'; *ted naraar*, 'by them'.

Possession

Possessive pronouns formed from the genitive (possessive) case forms of the personal and demonstrative pronouns are placed in front of the noun, eg *minii ner* (my name):

GRAMMAR

my	*minii*	our (ours not yours)	*bidnii*
your (inf)	*chinii*	our (ours and yours)	*manai*
your (sg)	*tany*	your (pl)	*tanai/ta naryn*
his/her/its	*tüünii*	their	*ted naryn*

You can also express possession with the suffixes of the comitative (*-tai*) or dative (*-d*) cases. The comitative case suffix is added to the object possessed, or the dative case suffix is added to the possessor:

a single room with a shower   *neg ortoi shürshüürtei öröö*
(lit: one bed-with shower-with room)

Do you have a hundred tugriks?   *tand zuun tögrög bainuu*
(lit: you-to hundred tugrik be?)

Verbs

The verb stem is the base form to which inflectional suffixes are attached. Dictionaries of Mongolian list verbs either as stems alone or as stems plus the suffix *-kh* which are like infinitives but are called present-future verbal nouns (see Tenses below):

to be   *bai-* or *baikh*
to go   *yav-* or *yavakh*
to give   *ög-* or *ögökh*

Commands & Requests

Commands and requests (imperative mood) expressed in the second person singular and plural are the same as the verb stem:

Come (here)!   *(naash) ir!* (stem of *irekh*)
Go away!   *zail* (stem of *zailakh*)

Negative commands are formed by placing the particles *bitgii* or *büü* ('don't') before the imperative:

Don't go!   *bitgii yav!*
Don't do it!   *büü khii!*

This rather abrupt tone can be softened by adding a suitable personal pronoun:

[You] please come here!   *ta naash ir!*
[You] please don't go! *chi bitgii yav!*

A polite or future request may be expressed with the future imperative (stem plus suffix *-aarai*):

Have a good journey!   *sain yav-**aa**rai!*
Please come in!   *or-**oo**roi!*
Come (tomorrow)!   *(margaash) ir-**ee**rei!*

You say 'I'll (do) ...' or 'let us (do) ...' with the stressed suffix *-i*:

I'll write!   *bich-**i**!*
Let's go!   *yav-**i**!*
Let me in!   *or-**i**!*

To Be
The word *bain* is the present-future tense form of *baikh* and means 'am', 'is' and 'are' (and also 'shall be' and 'will be'). Similarly, *baisan* means both 'was' and 'were':

I am/We are ready.   *bi/bid belen bain*
He was here for many months. *ter **o**lon sar end **ba**isan*

GRAMMAR

GRAMMAR

It is quite usual in Mongolian to omit the verb 'to be' from simple sentences of the 'Me Tarzan, you Jane' type:

I am a tourist.   *bi juulchin* (lit: 'I tourist')
He is a guide.   *ter khün gazarch* (lit: 'he guide')

While we say in English 'Do you have ...?' or 'Have you got ...?' the Mongols mostly ask 'Is there ...?' or 'Are there ...?' (*bainuu?*):

Have you got any change?   *zadgai möng bainuu?*

Some English phrases using 'to be' are expressed in Mongolian by other verb forms:

We are tired.   *bid yadarsan* (lit: we tired-became)
I'm thirsty.   *minii am tsangaj bain* (lit: my mouth thirsty-be)

Tenses
The tenses of the verb are embodied in a range of suffixes attached to the stem. For each tense of the verb there is one form which is the same for all persons singular and plural (the linking vowels following the rules of vowel harmony):

Present-Future
The present-future tense is formed with the suffix *-n :*

I am/we are ready	*bi/bid belen bain*
I go/I am going/I shall go	*bi yavan*
we go/we are going/we shall go	*bid yavan*
you give/you are giving/you shall give	*ta ögön*
they give/they are giving/they shall give	*ted nar ögön*

To emphasise that an action is taking place at the time of speaking, the present continuous tense is formed with the suffix -*j* (sometimes -*ch*), followed by the present/future tense of the verb to be':

| I am/We are going now. | *bi/bid odoo yavj bain* |
| You/They are giving. | *ta/ted nar ögch bain* |

To express an action taking place continuously over a long period, the suffix -*dag* (-*dög* etc) is added to the verb stem:

We (usually) go.	*bid yavdag*
You (regularly) give.	*ta ögdög*
I live in Ulan Bator city.	*bi Ulaanbaatar khotod suudag*

Sentences beginning with 'if' are formed by adding the suffix -*val* (-*völ* etc) to the verb stem; if the stem ends in -*v*, -*l* or -*m* the suffix is -*bal*, -*böl* etc:

| If we go ... | *bid yavbal* ... |
| If you give ... | *ta ögvöl* ... |

aival büü khii, khiivel büü ai
(proverb: If you're afraid don't do it, if you do it don't be afraid.)

Past
The past tense suffix -*v* indicates a completed action:

| We went. | *bid yavav* |
| You gave. | *ta ögöv* |

Completed actions are also shown by the perfective suffix *-san* (*-sön* etc), but it can be used more flexibly, eg:

We went.	*bid ya*vsan
You gave.	*ta ö*gsön
The man who went.	*ya*vsan khün
The money given.	*ö*gsön möng

Questions

Basic questions in Mongolian are formed by adding the particle *uu* (*üü*, *yuu*, *yüü*) at the end of the sentence, like a spoken question mark. The particle is written separately but pronounced as if it were part of the preceding word and stressed:

He's gone to Darkhan. *(ter khün) Darkhan khotod yavsan*
Has he gone to Darkhan? *(ter khün) Darkhan khotod yavsan***uu**?

When a sentence includes an interrogative (question word), however, *uu* is replaced by *ve* (*be* after *-v*, *-m* and *-n*):

what	*yuu*
what kind of	*yamar*
when	*khezee*
where	*khaan*
where to	*khaashaa*
where from	*khaanaas*
who	*khen*
whose	*khenii*

What is this? *en yuu ve?*
What kind of room have you got? *yamar öröötei yum be?*

When will you come?	*ta khezee irekh ve?*
Where is he/she?	*ter khaan bain ve?*
Where are you going?	*ta khaashaa yavj bain ve?*
Where have you come from?	*ta khaanaas irsen be?*
Who is in there?	*tend khen bain ve?*
Whose book is this?	*en khenii nom be?*

The *-ve/be* is stressed, and the verb (*bain*) may be omitted. Note the doubling of the question words for the plural:

What is (what things are) in there?	*tend yuu yuu bain ve?*
Who is (which people are) in there?	*tend khen khen bain ve?*
Whose books are these?	*en khen khenii nom be?*

The question 'how?' eg how to do something, uses forms of the verb *yaakh,* 'to do what?' which has no English equivalent:

How can it be done?	*üüniig yaaj khiikh ve?*
What's the matter?	*yaaj bain?*

On its own *yaakh ve* (often pronounced yaakhev) means 'What is to be done?', but as an exclamation it means 'Never mind!' Another form of the same verb, *yaagaad,* means 'why?':

Why did that happen?   *yaagaad iim bolov?*

The Mongolian for 'how', in combinations like 'how far?', 'how much?', 'how many?' etc, and for 'which?' depends on the context:

How far is it?	*ail kher khol ve?*
How much is it?	*en yamar üntei ve?*
How much do you need?	*khed kheregtei ve?*

How (many years) old are you (inf)? *chi kheden nastai ve?*
Which man?   *yamar khün be?*

Yes & No

The Mongolian for 'yes' is *tiim* (emphatic: *tiimee*), which means 'just so'. Quite often however Mongols answer in the affirmative by repeating the key word (noun or verb) in the question for emphasis. 'No' is *ügüi* (lit: lack). This is contracted to *-güi* as a negative suffix for both nouns and verbs meaning 'not' or 'without'. A simple negative answer consists of the key word plus the negative suffix, although verb tense forms may vary:

Do you have a hat?   *ta malgaitai yuu?*
Yes (I have).   *malgaitai, malgaitai*
Has he gone to Darkhan?   *(ter khün) Darkhan khotod yavsanuu?*
Yes (he has).   *yavsan*
No (he hasn't).   *yavsangüi or yavaagüi*
No (he's not going).   *yavakhgüi*

When you mean 'not this one (but that one)' you say *en bish*.

Postpositions

English prepositions like 'to', 'towards', 'on', 'near', 'with', 'before', 'after' etc stand after the nouns they refer to in Mongolian and may require the noun stems to take a suffix:

towards	*ruu (rüü)*	together	*khamt*
there	*tiish*	before	*ömön*
on/above	*deer*	after	*daraa*
near	*derged*	behind	*khoish*

GRAMMAR

to (the) town	*khot ruu*
to the left/right	*züün/baruun tiish*
on the table	*shireen deer*
near the door	*üüdnii derged*
(together) with you	*tantai khamt*
before food	*khoolny ömön*
after food	*khoolny daraa*
after me	*nadaas khoish*

Note *khoishoo!* – Push off!

Postpositions themselves may have suffixes:

from above	*deerees*
	(*deer*, 'above' + long vowel + *s*: 'from')
in that direction	*tiishee*
	(tiish, 'there' + long vowel: 'towards')
on my behalf	*minii ömnöös*
	(*minii*, 'my' + *ömön*, 'before' + long vowel + *s*: 'from')

Nouns with case suffixes (see page 19) are sometimes sufficient to convey the same idea without postpositions :

from Australia	*Avstrali Ulsaas*
by air (mail)	*agaaraar*
with him	*tüüntei*

Comparison

Which one is better?	*alin deer ve?*
This one is better.	*enen ilüü*
a bit better	*arai deer*

a bit worse	*arai muu*
a bit more	*arai ilüü*
a bit less	*arai bag*
a bit quicker	*arai khurdan*

Comparison between two objects is made by attaching the ablative case suffix (long vowel + *s* meaning 'from') to the object noun immediately before the adjective (a verb may not be needed):

London is bigger than Ulan Bator.
   London Ulaanbaataraas tom
This room is smaller than that one.
   en öröö ter öröönöös jijig
Today's lights are better than tomorrow's lard.
   margaashiin öökhnöös önöödriin uushig deer (roughly the equivalent of 'a bird in the hand ...' – the Mongols have a high regard for animal fat)

Note that 'please have some more' in Mongolian is *ta dakhiad av* (lit: please take again).

The superlative is easily formed with the help of the noun *khamag* ('all', 'everything') in the genitive (possessive) case (suffix in -*iin*):

the biggest	*khamgiin tom*
the smallest	*khamgiin jijig*

Quantity

all	*bükh*
a bit	*jaakhan*
enough	*khangalttai*

every	*tutam*
everybody	*khün bür*
everything	*yum bügd*
few	*tsöön*
less	*dutuu*
little	*bag*
many	*olon*
more	*ilüü*
much	*ikh*
several	*kheden*

Some Useful Words

about	*orchin*
almost	*barag*
altogether	*niitdee*
and	*ba*
because	*uchraas*
beforehand	*uirdaas*
but	*kharin*
if possible	*chadakh chineegeer*
if so	*khervee tiim bol*
otherwise (alternatively)	*esvel*

GRAMMAR

Greetings & Civilities

Greetings

The all-purpose ritual greeting in Mongolia is:

Hello!
sain bainuu!   Сайн байна уу?

This means literally 'Are you well?' and is used when we might say 'How do you do?' or 'How are you?' The invariable response is:

Fine. How are you?
sain ta sain bainuu?   Сайн. Та сайн байна уу?

You then answer that you are fine, too:

Fine!
sain bainaa!   Сайн байнаа!
What's new?
sonin saikhan yuu bain?   Сонин сайхан юу байна?

The universal response to this question is:

Nothing really. (lit: 'It's peaceful.')
taivan bain   Тайван байна.

If you are visiting a family, especially in the country, having agreed that everybody's fine you should proceed to asking about family members and livestock and only then to more general matters:

How is your family?
  tanaikhan sainuu?   Танайхан сайн уу?
I hope your animals are
fattening up nicely?
  mal süreg targan tavtaiyuu? Мал сүрэг тарган тавтай юу?

The answer you expect to the last question is:

Fattening nicely!
  tavtai saikhan!   Тавтай сайхан!

These initial questions are not intended to elicit specific answers; they are expressions of goodwill. Such ritual questions and responses are considered quite natural and necessary when nomads offer hospitality to strangers. The host may respond by saying that he hopes the visitor's wishes will come true:

May it be so!
  boltugai!   Болтугай!
May your wish come true!
  yöröölöör bolog!   Ерөөлөөр болог!

Other possible questions and answers include:

Are you very busy?
  ta ikh zavgüi bainuu?   Та их завгүй байна уу?

How are things? (How's work and everything?)	
ajil üils sainuu?	Ажил үйлс сайн уу?
Not bad.	
muugüi	Муугүй.
And you?	
tanaar yuu bain?	Танаар юу байна?
Nothing special.	
onts goid yumgüi	Онц гойд юмгүй.

Goodbyes

It's time to go.	
yavakh tsag bolchikhood bain	Явах цаг болчихоод байна.
We had a good time.	
saikhan bolloo	Сайхан боллоо.
Goodbye.	
bayartai	Баяртай.
Good night. (Sleep well!)	
saikhan untaarai	Сайхан унтаарай.
See you tomorrow!	
margaash uulzii!	Маргааш уулзая!
See you later!	
daraa uulzii!	Дараа уулзая!
Come again soon.	
dakhiad ireerei	Дахиад ирээрэй.

The Mongolian for 'bon voyage' literally means 'go well!':

Safe journey!	
sain yavaarai	Сайн яваарай!

GREETINGS

The response from those leaving to those staying is:

Stay well!
   sain suuj baigaarai!   Сайн сууж байгаарай!

For the equivalent of 'All the best!' (or if you sign off a letter or note) you can say:

Wishing you all good things!
   sain saikhan bükhniig   Сайн сайхан бүхнийг
   yörööi!   ерөөе!

The more formal written 'Yours sincerely' is Хүндэтгэн ёслогч.

Civilities

The Mongols have no special word for 'please', the degree of politeness of a request being reflected in the verb form of address used (see Grammar chapter). There are several ways of saying 'thank you', including:

Thanks.	*bayarlaa/gyalailaa*	Баярлалаа/Гялайлаа.
Thank you very much.	*tand ikh bayarlaa*	Танд их баярлалаа.
Much obliged.	*bayarlalgüi yaakhev?*	Баярлалгүй яах вэ?

If someone has done you a favour, a polite response is:

Thank you for your hospitality.
   saikhan zochluullaa   Сайхан зочлууллаа!
Thank you for your help.
   ta ikh tus bolloo!   Та их тус боллоо!
Not at all/Don't mention it.
   zügeer   Зүгээр.

GREETINGS

GREETINGS

Requests

I'd like to ask you a favour.
tanaas neg yum khüsi

Танаас нэг юм хүсье!

May I ask you a question?
*tanaas neg yum asuuj
bolokhuu?*

Танаас нэг юм асууж
болох уу?

Please help me if you can.
ta khicheej tus bolooch

Та хичээж тус болооч!

Please could you repeat that?
*ta dakhiad neg khelj
ögökhgüiyüü?*

Та дахиад нэг хэлж
өгөхгүй юү?

Please show me that.
tüüniig nad üzüüleech

Түүнийг над үзүүлээч!

Will you pass it to me, please?
*naadakhygaa avaad
ögnüü?*

Наадахыгаа аваад
өгнө үү?

Can I take ... now?
bi odoo ... avakhuu?

Би одоо ... авах уу?

May I go now?
bi odoo yavj bolokhuu?

Би одоо явж болох уу?

Please don't forget!
ta bitgii martaarai!

Та битгий мартаарай!

Apologies

I'm sorry/Excuse me!
uuchlaarai!

Уучлаарай!

I beg your pardon!
örshöögöörei!

Өршөөгөөрэй!

It's all my fault.
miniil buruu bolloo

Миний л буруу боллоо!

It doesn't matter.

    khamaagüi   Хамаагүй.

Don't mention it.

    zügeer   Зүгээр.

Sorry? What (did you say)?

    yuu genee?   Юу гэнээ?

Names

Mongols have just one given name (*ner*) which serves as both forename and surname. Short or familiar forms of the given name are used within the family or among close friends. Wives do not adopt their husband's name on marriage.

Mongolian names for men often denote 'manly' qualities, like *Bat* (strong), *Bold* (steel), *Chuluun* (stone) or *Sükh* (axe). Women may be named after flowers, like *Narantsetseg* (sunflower), *Udval* (chrysanthemum) or *Khongorzul* (thistle), or qualities like *Oyuun* (wisdom). Some personal names are of Tibetan origin or have come from Sanskrit via Lamaism, including *Dorjpalam* (diamond) and *Ochir* and *Bazar* (both meaning *vajra* or thunderbolt), while *Lianhua* (lotus) and *Lookhuuz* ('old man with a beard') are Chinese. In modern times Mongols have sometimes been given Russian names like *Vladimir, Sasha, Oktiabr* (October) and *Seseer* (USSR). The name *Chinges* (Genghis Khan) is not used, however.

To distinguish themselves from others with the same given name, Mongols precede it with their father's name (sometimes their mother's) plus a possessive suffix – *Bat-yn Dorj, Dorj-iin Dulmaa*, etc, where Dorj's father's name is Bat and Dulmaa's father's name is Dorj. The Mongols call their father's name (patronymic) *ovog*, which originally meant 'clan'. It is often reduced to the initial letter – *B. Dorj, D. Dulmaa*, etc. When they write their patronymics in English some Mongols omit the possessive suffix – *Bat Dorj, Dorj Dulmaa*. Mongols from Russia have adopted full Russian name forms – given name, patronymic and inherited surname.

What's your name?
  tany ner khen be?   Таны нэр хэн бэ?
My name is Bold.
  minii ner Bold   Миний нэр Болд.
What's yours?
  tany ner?   Таны нэр?
What's your full name (name
and patronymic)?
  tany ovog neriig khen   Таны овог нэрийг хэн
  gedeg ve?   гэдэг вэ?
My full name is Chuluuny
Bold.
  minii ovog ner Chuluuny   Миний овог нэр Чулууны
  Bold   Болд.

Forms of Address

Mongols address one another by name, relationship or job title plus the word *guai*, which is polite, or an appropriate long vowel, forming a vocative:

Hey, Bat!
  bataa!   Бат аа!
Dorj!
  dorjoo!   Дорж оо!
Mr Dorj!
  dorj guai!   Дорж гуай!
Mrs/Miss Dulmaa!
  dulmaa guai!   Дулмаа гуай!

Dad!
  aavaa!   Аав аа!
Waiter!
  zöögchöö!   Зөөгч өө!
Excuse me, sir/madam!
  khün guai!   Хүн гуай!
My child! (to a young person)
  khüükhee!   Хүүх ээ!

People in authority are addressed as *khündet* or *erkhemseg*
('esteemed'):

Mr Chairman!
  khündet daragaa!   Хүндэт дарга аа!
Your Excellency! (to an
ambassador)
  erkhemseg elchin saidaa! Эрхэмсэг элчин сайд аа!

Foreign men are addressed as *noyon* ('mister', originally a prince,
and the king in chess), and women as *khatagtai*:

Mr Smith!
  noyon smit!   Ноён Смит!
Mrs/Miss Smith!
  khatagtai smit!   Хатагтай Смит!
Ladies and gentlemen!
  noyod khatagtai naraa!   Ноёд хатагтай нар аа!

During the communist period of Mongolia's history members of
the ruling party were called 'comrade' *(nökhör)*. The term was
extended to non-communists as the common form of address,
but is now going out of fashion.

GREETINGS

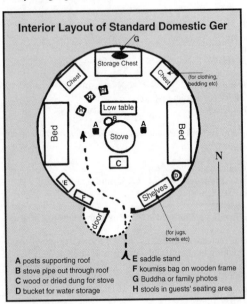

Interior Layout of Standard Domestic Ger

A posts supporting roof
B stove pipe out through roof
C wood or dried dung for stove
D bucket for water storage
E saddle stand
F koumiss bag on wooden frame
G Buddha or family photos
H stools in guests' seating area

Body Language

Your host will usually meet you outside his *ger* and invite you in. On entering, don't step on the threshold. Once inside move round the stove in a clockwise direction. As seen from the place of honour at the back (north side) of the *ger*, looking towards the door (south), Mongol men sit to the right (west) and women to the left (east). The host will show you a place appropriate to your status, age and sex (see In the Country, page 87). Sit on the stool provided or sit or squat on the floor (carpet), tucking your feet under yourself rather than sticking your legs out. You shouldn't lean against the *ger* wall or furniture.

Bowls of food and drink are offered to guests by the hostess in both hands, or in the right hand supported by the left at the elbow, and are received in the right hand. The host may sprinkle a little tea or vodka from his bowl as an oblation to bring good luck to his hearth. Don't throw anything into the fire yourself. The giving and receiving of gifts is done standing, with both hands. Mongols appreciate efforts to share their customs, but they don't expect foreigners to know much about them.

Some movements and gestures will be familiar – nodding the head from side to side to mean doubt or refusal, scratching the back of the head to mean uncertainty, and thumbs up (right thumb) to express approval. To wave your sleeve is a mark of protest, and extending the little finger of your right hand is a sign of dissatisfaction.

Mongols living in the countryside are not used to shaking hands with visitors, but most townspeople are familiar with this and other foreign customs learned from the Russians. Mongols always dress and behave modestly. Drunks in Mongolia, like most other places, are more a nuisance than a threat.

GREETINGS

Small Talk

In Ulan Bator most Mongols are used to seeing Europeans and are not particularly curious about them, other than to sell them something! In the countryside visitors are the focus of curiosity and your arrival will be treated as a big event. Country Mongols are very observant, and even as your hosts are offering hospitality in the family *ger*, neighbours from miles around who will have noticed a strange vehicle or simply seen your dust-cloud will be riding in to look you over.

Be prepared for personal questions, about your age, wages and family circumstances, but don't expect people to have any clear idea about where you're from. How many livestock does your country have per head of the human population?!

Some Mongols still assume that European visitors must be Russian, although most of the Russians who used to work in Mongolia have gone home. Some Mongols mistrust Russia and China because of the way Mongolia was treated by them, and they are wary of people from these countries.

Meeting People
Say 'hello' to people with the traditional *sain bainuu* (see the Greetings & Civilities chapter).

What's your name?
tany ner khen be?   Таны нэр хэн бэ?
My name is Bold.
minii ner Bold   Миний нэр Болд.
What's yours?

My name is ...
minii ner ...   Миний нэр ...

Nationalities

What country are you from?
ta yamar ulsaas irsen be?   Та ямар улсаас ирсэн бэ?

I'm from ...	*bi ... ulsaas irsen*	Би ... улсаас ирсэн.
Argentina	*Argentin*	Аргентин
Australia	*Avstrali*	Австрали
Austria	*Avstri*	Австри
Britain	*Ikh Britani*	Их Британи
Canada	*Kanad*	Канад
China	*Khyatad*	Хятад
Egypt	*Misir*	Мисир
England	*Angil*	Англи
France	*Frants*	Франц
Germany	*German*	Герман
India	*Enetkheg*	Энэтхэг
Iran	*Iran*	Иран
Ireland	*Irland*	Ирланд
Italy	*Itali*	Итали
Japan	*Yapon*	Япон
Korea	*Solongos*	Солонгос
Mexico	*Meksik*	Мексик
New Zealand	*Shin Zeland*	Шинэ Зеланд

SMALL TALK

Norway	*Norvegi*	Норвеги
Singapore	*Singapor*	Сингапор
South Africa	*Ömnöd Afrik*	Өмнөд Африк
Sweden	*Shved*	Швед
Switzerland	*Shvetsari*	Швецари
Taiwan	*Taivang*	Тайван
the USA	*Amerikiin Negdsen*	Америкийн Нэгдсэн

If you're from Hong Kong you say *bi gongkongoos irsen*.

What town are you from?
   ta ail khotoos irsen be?   Та аль хотоос ирсэн бэ?
I'm from the town of ...
   bi ... khotoos irsen   Би ... хотоос ирсэн.
Where is that?
   khaan baidag bilee?   Хаана байдаг билээ?
Please show me.
   nadad zaaj ögööch   Надад зааж өгөөч!
I came by plane.
   bi nisekh ongotsoor irsen   Би нисэх онгоцоор ирсэн.
I came by train.
   bi galt tergeer irsen   Би галт тэргээр ирсэн.

Age

How old are you?
   ta kheden nastai ve?   Та хэдэн настай вэ?

I am ... years old.	*bi ... nastai*	Би ... настай.
18	*arvan naiman*	арван найман
25	*khorin tavan*	хорин таван

See the Numbers chapter for your particular age.

wrestler
böh
бөх

Occupations

What do you do?
 ta yamar ajil khiideg ve? Та ямар ажил хийдэг вэ?

I'm a/an...	*bi ...*	Би ...
actor	*jüjigchin*	жүжигчин
artist	*zuraach*	зураач
business person	*naimaachin*	наймаачин
doctor	*emch*	эмч
driver	*jolooch*	жолооч
engineer	*injener*	инженер
journalist	*setgüülch*	сэтгүүлч
lawyer	*khuuilch*	хуульч

manual worker	*ajilchin*	ажилчин
mechanic	*mekhanik*	механик
musician	*khögjimchin*	хөгжимчин
nurse	*suvilagch*	сувилагч
office worker	*ajiltan*	ажилтан
politician	*uls töriyn zütgelten*	уис төрийн зутгэлтзн
scientist	*sudlaach*	судлаач
secretary	*bicheech*	бичээч
student	*oyuutan*	оюутан
teacher	*bagsh*	багш
waiter	*üilchlegch*	үйлчлэгч
writer	*zokhiolch*	зохиолч

Where do you work?
   ta khaan ajilladag ve?   Та хаана ажилладаг вэ?

I work ...	*bi ... ajilladag*	Би ... ажилладаг.
for the army	*tsergiin alband*	цэргийн албанд
for a bank	*bankind*	банкинд
for a company	*kompanid*	компанид
in a factory	*üildvert*	үйлдвэрт
for the government	*zasgiin gazart*	засгийн газарт
at home	*gertee*	гэртээ
in a hospital	*emnelegt*	эмнэлэгт
in a library	*nomyn sangd*	номын санд
in a school	*surguuild*	сургуульд
in a university	*ikh surguuild*	их сургуульд

I've come ...	*bi ... irsen*	Би ... ирсэн.
on business	*bizneseer*	бизнэсээр
on holiday	*amraltaar*	амралтаар

SMALL TALK

to learn Mongolian	*mongol khel*	монгол хэл
to study	*surakhaar*	сурахаар
to study	*surakhaar*	сурахаар
to work	*ajillakhaar*	ажиллахаар

Gandang Monastery

Religion

What is your religion?
ta yamar shashintai ve?   Та ямар шашинтай вэ?

I am ...	*bi ... shashintan*	Би ... шашинтан.
Buddhist	*buddyn*	буддын
Catholic	*katolik*	католик
Christian	*khristosyn/khristiin*	христосын/христийн
Hindu	*khindüün*	хиндүүн
Jewish	*yevrein/iudei*	еврейн/иудей
Muslim	*lalyn*	лалын
Protestant	*protestant*	протестант
shamanist	*böögiin*	бөөгийн

I'm not religious.
bi shashin shütdeggüi khün Би шашин шүтдэггүй хүн.

SMALL TALK

Family

Are you married?
ta urgalsanuu?
Та урагласан уу?

No, I'm not.
ügüi, bi urgalaagüi
Үгүй, би ураглаагүй

I'm single.
bi gants bii
Би ганц бие.

Yes, I am/I'm married.
tiimee, bi urgalsan
Тиймээ, би урагласан.

Is your husband/wife also here?
tany nökhör/ekhner end baigaa yuu?
Таны нөхөр/эхнэр энд байгаа юу?

Do you have any children?
ta khüükhedteiyüü?
Та хүүхэдтэй юу?

Yes, one/two.
tiimee, neg/khoyor
Тиймээ, нэг/хоёр.

Yes, three/four.
tiimee, gurav/döröv
Тиймээ, гурав/дөрөв.

How many children do you have?
ta kheden khüükhedtei ve?
Та хэдэн хүүхэдтэй вэ?

I have a daughter/son.
bi okhintoi/khüütei
Би охинтой/хүүтэй.

I don't have any children.
bi yeröösöö khüükhedgüi
Би ерөөсөө хүүхэдгүй.

How many brothers and sisters do you have?
ta kheden düütei ve?
Та хэдэн дүүтэй вэ?

I don't have any brothers or sisters.
nadad düü baikhgüi
Надад дүү байхгүй

Do you have a boyfriend?
   ta eregtei naiztaiyuu?   Та эрэгтэй найзтай юу?
Do you have a girlfriend?
   ta emegtei naiztaiyuu?   Та эмэгтэй найзтай юу?
Yes.
   tiim   Тийм.
No.
   ügüi   Үгүй.

Family Members

mother	*eej*	ээж
father	*aav*	аав
son	*khüü*	хүү
daughter	*okhin*	охин
elder brother	*akh*	ах
elder sister	*egch*	эгч
younger brother/sister	*düü*	дүү
husband	*nökhör*	нөхөр
wife	*ekhner*	эхнэр

Feelings

I am ...	*bi ... bain*	Би ... байна.
angry	*uurlaj*	уурлаж
cold	*daarch*	даарч
happy	*bayartai*	баяртай
hot	*khaluutsaj*	халууцаж
hungry	*ölsöj*	өлсөж
in a hurry	*yaarch*	яарч
sleepy	*noirmogloj*	нойрмоглож
thirsty	*tsangaj*	цангаж
tired	*yadarch*	ядарч

SMALL TALK

I am sorry!
  uuchlaarai!   Уучлаарай!
I am grateful.
  bayarlaa!   Баярлалаа!

Opinions

Do you like ...?   *ta ... durtai yuu?*   Та ... дуртай юу?
  Mongolian ...   *mongolyn ...*   монголын ...
  Western ...   *baruuny ...*   барууны ...
  Chinese ...   *khyatadyn ...*   хятадын ...
  Russian ...   *orosyn ...*   оросын ...
  ... books   *... nomd*   ... номд
  ... films   *... kinond*   ... кинонд
  ... food   *... khoolond*   ... хоолонд
  ... music   *... khögjimd*   ... хөгжимд
  travelling   *ayalald*   аялалд

I like ...
  bi ... durtai   Би ... дуртай.
I don't like ...
  bi ... durgüi   Би ... дургүй.
Very interesting!
  ikh sonin bain!   Их сонин байна.
Really?
  neereniüü?   Нээрэн үү?
Do you agree?
  ta zövshöörch bainuu?   Та зөвшөөрч байна уу?
I don't agree.
  bi zövshöörökhgüi   Би зөвшөөрөхгүй.

Language Difficulties

I don't speak Mongol.
   bi mongoloor yairdaggüi   Би монголоор ярьдаггүй.

Do you speak English?
   ta angilar yairdaguu?   Та англиар ярьдаг уу?

Would you say that again?
   ta terniig dakhiad kheleed   Та тэрнийг дахиад хэлээд
   ögööch   өгөөч.

Could you speak more
slowly?
   ta jaal udaan yarinuu?   Та жаал удаан ярина уу?

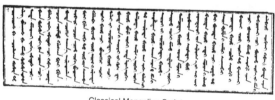

Classical Mongolian Script

Please point to the phrase in
the book.
   yariany nom deer zaaj   Ярианы ном дээр зааж
   ögööch   өгөөч!

Let me see if I can find it in
this book.
   bi en nom deer oloodkhi   Би энэ ном дээр олоодхоё.

I understand.
   bi oilgoj bain   Би ойлгож байна.

I don't understand.
   bi oilgokhgüi bain   Би ойлгохгүй байна.

SMALL TALK

What does this mean?
  en yamar utagtai ve?   Энэ ямар утгатай вэ?

Some Useful Phrases

Can I take a photo?
  bi zurag avch bolokh uu?   Би зураг авч болох уу?
Sure.
  bololgüi yaakhev   Бололгүй яах вэ.
What is this/that called?
  üüniig/tüüniig yuu gedeg   Үүнийг/түүнийг юу гэдэг
  yum be?   юм бэ?
Do you live here?
  ta end aimdardaguu?   Та энд амьдардаг уу?
Yes, I live here.
  tiimee bi end aimdardag   Тийм ээ, би энд амьдардаг.
No, I don't live here.
  ügüi bi end aimdardaggüi   Үгүй, би энд амьдардаггүй.

SMALL TALK

Getting Around

The Mongolian national tourist organisation Juulchin naturally is happy to arrange hotel accommodation and visits to Mongolia's chief attractions for tour groups at a price. Because of the shortage of planes and fuel, buying tickets for internal flights is difficult and requires forward planning. Mongolia is a big and empty place without proper roads and there is no regular vehicle traffic in country areas. Where and when you can travel without an expensive organised tour depends on how good you are at bargaining and on the availability of jeeps, drivers and petrol, or horses and guides, from private travel agencies or freelance operators.

What times does the	*kheden tsagt ...*	Хэдэн цагт ...
... leave/arrive?	*yavakh/irekh ve?*	явах/ирэх вэ?
bus	*avtobus*	автобус
trolleybus	*trolleibus*	троллейбус
train	*galt tereg*	галт тэрэг
plane	*nisekh ongots*	нисэх онгоц

How can I get to ...?
   bi ... yaaj yavakh ve?   Би ... яаж явах вэ?
How much is it to go to ...?
   ... yavakhad yamar üntei ve? ... явахад ямар үнэтэй вэ?

53

Is there another way to get
there?
  *tiishee yavakh öör zam
  biiyüü?*   Тийшээ явах өөр зам
                    бий юу?

Finding Your Way

Where is the ...?   *... khaan bain ve?*   ... хаана байна вэ?

train station	*galt tergenii buudal*	Галт тэрэгний буудал
bus station	*avtobusny buudal*	Автобусны буудал
bus stop	*avtobusny zogsool*	Автобусны зогсоол
trolleybus stop	*trolleibusny zogsool*	троллейбусны зогсоол
airport	*nisekh ongotsny buudal*	Нисэх онгоцны буудал
ticket office	*biletiin kass*	Билетийн касс

What ... is this?	*en yamar ... ve?*	Энэ ... ямар вэ?
square	*talbai*	талбай
street	*gudamj*	гудамж
suburb	*düüreg*	дүүрэг

Is it far?
  kholuu?   Хол уу?
Yes, it's far.
  tiimee khol   Тиймээ, хол.
No, it's not far.
  ügüi khol bish   Үгүй, хол биш.
Is it near here?
  endees oirkhonuu?   Эндээс ойрхон уу?

Can I walk there?
 bi tüshee yavgan yavj
 bolokhuu?

Би тийшээ явган явж
болох уу?

Is it difficult to find?
 olokhod khetsüüyüü?

Олоход хэцүү юу?

Excuse me, what direction
is ...?
 uuchlaarai ... ail zügt
 bain ve?

Уучлаарай, аль зүгт
 байна вэ?

Excuse me, am I going in the
right direction for ...?
 uuchlaarai bi ... ruu zöv
 yavj bainuu?

Уучлаарай, би ... руу зөв
явж байна уу?

Where is the toilet?
 jorlong khaan baidag ve?

Жорлон хаана байдаг вэ?

Directions

It's useful to know your compass points. Outside central Ulan
Bator homes and offices have no street address, their location
being described with reference to some local landmark,
eg second east-side entrance of the *ger* compound north of the
State Department Store'. Fortunately, Bogd Khan mountain, situ-
ated directly south of the city, is usually visible from most places
for orientation.

khoid/umard   N   хойд/умард

baruun/örnöd   W   E   *züün/doron*
баруун/өрнөд   зүүн/дорно

urd/ömön   S   урд/өмнө

behind/after	*khoin/ard*	хойно/ард
in front/before	*ömön*	өмнө
to the left	*baruun tiish*	баруун тийш
to the right	*züün tiish*	зүүн тийш
straight ahead	*chigeeree*	чигээрээ
up(stairs)	*deeshee*	дээшээ
down(stairs)	*dooshoo*	доошоо

For more directions see the In the Country chapter, page 86.

Air

Mongolia's airline MIAT (Mongolian Civil Aviation Co) flies once or twice a week to several cities in the Russian Federation, China and Kazakhstan as well as tourist centres and provincial towns in Mongolia. Popular tourist destinations include South Gobi camp (desert sands and camels), Kharkhorin or Khujirt (Erdenezuu monastery and the ruins of the ancient capital Karakorum) and Khovd (hunting and mountaineering). Children aged 5 to 16 are half-price. Foreigners pay in dollars. Excess baggage charges can be painful.

When is the next flight to ...?
    ... ruu yavakh daraagiin nisleg khezee ve?
    ... руу явах дараагийн нислэг хэзээ вэ?
How long does the flight take?
    kheden tsag nisekh ve?
    Хэдэн цаг нисэх вэ?
I would like to book a ticket to ...
    bi ... ruu yavakh bilet bürtgüülekh gesen yum
    Би ... руу явах билет бүртгүүлэх гэсэн юм.

Is this the flight to ...?
en ... ruu yavakh nislegüü?   Энэ ... руу явах нислэг үү?

Please show your ...	*ta ... üzüülenüü*	Та ... үзүүлнэ үү?
boarding pass	*suukh talonaa*	суух талонаа
customs declaration	*gaaliin*	гаалийн
	todorkhoiloltoo	тодорхойлолтоо
passport	*pasportoo*	паспортоо

book	*bürtgüülekh*	бүртгүүлэх
cancel	*bolikh*	болих
confirm	*batalgaajuulakh*	баталгаажуулах
standard-class ticket	*engiin bilet*	энгийн билет
1st-class ticket	*negdügeer*	нэгдүгээр
	zergiin bilet	зэргийн билет
smoking	*tamikh tatdag*	тамхи татдаг
nonsmoking	*tamikh tatdaggüi*	тамхи татаггүй

Bus

Central Ulan Bator is served by bus and trolleybus routes but demand far exceeds supply and overcrowding is usual. Most routes have conductors who sell a one-price ticket for cash. Season tickets are available, and sometimes route maps in English. Small towns without buses have flat-rate 'fixed-route taxi' *(marshrutyn taksi)* services by minibus *(mikroavtobus)* – pay the driver. Inter-city bus services have been infrequent and expensive since petrol supplies became irregular.

Does this bus go to ...?
  en avtobus ... ruu
  yavdaguu?

Энэ автобус ... руу явдагуу?

Which bus goes to ...?
  ... ruu yamar avtobus
  yavdag ve?

... руу ямар автобус явдаг вэ?

How frequently do the buses run?
  avtobus ail kher olon
  udaa yavdag ve?

Автобус аль хэр олон удаа явдаг вэ?

Can you tell me when we get to ...?
  ta nadad bid khezee ... deer
  ochikhyg khelj ögööch?

Та надад бид хэзээ ... дээр очихыг хэлж өгөөч?

I want to get off!
  bi buumaar bain!

Би буумаар байна!

Please let me off at the next stop.
  namaig daraagiin buudal
  deer buulgaj ögööch

Намайг дараагийн буудал дээр буулгаж өгөөч.

Please open the doors!
  khaalag ongoilgooroi!

Хаалга онгойлгоорой!

The popular name for an Ulan Bator trolleybus is 'goat cart' (*yamaa tereg*), because the poles look like a goat's horns.

When is the ... bus? ... *avtobus khezee ve?*   автобус хэзээ вэ?
next   *daraagiin*   Дараагийн
first   *ekhnii*   Эхний
last   *süüliin*   Сүүлийн

Train

International train services between Moscow and Peking pass through Mongolia once a week, stopping at Ulan Bator, Darkhan and one or two other towns, including Sükhbaatar and Zamyn-Üüd for border and customs controls. There is also a once-weekly service between Peking and Ulan Bator. International train services are always packed and it is necessary to book months in

advance. There are de luxe and standard classes in Russian trains and soft and hard in Chinese trains, the equivalent of 1st and 2nd class. At the time of writing you couldn't buy return tickets. Mongolian local trains run to Sükhbaatar, Erdenet, Bagnuur, Choir and Sainshand several times a week, and twice-daily 'commuter' services link Ulan Bator with nearby settlements like Züünkharaa and Nalaikh.

Does the train go to ...?
   ... ruu galt tereg yavdag uu?   ... руу галт тэрэг явдаг уу?

Do I need to change?
bi galt tergee solikh yostoi yuu?

Би галт тэргээ солих ёстой юу?

When does the train leave?
galt tereg kheden tsagt khödlökh ve?

Галт тэрэг хэдэн цагт хөдлөх вэ?

Buying Tickets

Excuse me, where is the ticket office?
uuchlaarai biletiin kass khaan bain ve?

Уучлаарай, билетийн касс хаана байна вэ?

I would like a ticket to ...
bi ... ruu yavakh neg tasalbar avmaar bain

Би ... руу явах нэг тасалбар авмаар байна.

I would like to reserve a seat.
bi neg suudal zakhialmaar bain

Би нэг суудал захиалмаар байна.

How much is it?
en yamar üntei ve?

Энэ ямар үнэтэй вэ?

How much is a berth in the sleeping car?
untlagynkh yamar üntei ve?

Унтлагынх ямар үнэтэй вэ?

Some Useful Phrases

Please show me your ticket.
ta tasalbaraa üzüülenüü?
Та тасалбараа үзүүлнэ үү?

I would like to upgrade my ticket.
bi biletee öörchilmöör bain
Би билетээ өөрчилмөөр байна.

I've lost my ticket.
bi tasalbaraa geechikhlee
Би тасалбараа гээчихлээ.

This ticket is not valid.
en bilet khüchingüi boljee
Энэ билет хүчингүй болжээ.

Is this seat taken?
en suudal khüntei yüü?
Энэ суудал хүнтэй юү?

Excuse me, this is my seat.
uuchlaarai en minii suudal
Уучлаарай, энэ миний суудал.

Where are we now?
bid odoo khaan bain ve?
Бид одоо хаана байна вэ?

What is this station called?
en buudlyg yuu gedeg ve?
Энэ буудлыг юу гэдэг вэ?

What is the next station?
daraagiin buudal yamar buudal ve?
Дараагийн буудал ямар буудал вэ?

I want to go to ...
bi ... ruu yavmaar bain
Би ... руу явмаар байна.

Can you tell me when we get there?
bid khezee khürekhiig khelj ögnüü?
Бид хэзээ хүрэхийг хэлж өгнө үү?

I want to get off at ...
bi ... deer buukh gesen yum
Би ... дээр буух гэсэн юм.

Some Useful Words

adult's ticket	*tom khünii tasalbar*	том хүний тасалбар
child's ticket	*khüükhdiin tasalbar*	хүүхдийн тасалбар
dining car	*vagon restoran*	вагон ресторан
no smoking	*tamikh tatdaggüi*	тамхи татдаггүй
railway station	*galt tergenii buudal*	галт тэрэгний буудал
single (single) ticket	*neg talyn bilet*	нэг талын билет
return (round trip) ticket	*khoyor talyn bilet*	хоёр талын билет
1st class	*negdügeer zereg*	нэгдүгээр зэрэг
2nd class	*khoyordugaar zereg*	хоёрдугаар зэрэг
de luxe	*lyuks*	люкс
standard	*engiin*	энгийн
soft	*zöölön suudal*	зөөлөн суудал
hard	*khatuu suudal*	хатуу суудал
sleeper	*untlagyn suudal*	унтлагын суудал
train	*galt tereg*	галт тэрэг
ticket	*tasalbar/bilet*	тасалбар/билет
timetable	*tsagiin khuvaair*	цагийн хуваарь

Taxi

Where can I get a taxi?
   bi khaanaas taksi   Би хаанаас такси
   avch bolokh ve?   авч болох вэ?
Are you free?
   ta sul bainuu?   Та сул байна уу?

Would you take me ...	*ta namaig ...* *khürgej ögnüü?*	Та намайг ... хүргэж өгнүү?
to this address	*en khayagaar*	энэ хаягаар
to the ... hotel	*... zochid buudald*	... зочид буудалд

Can you wait for me?
namaig khüleej
baikhgüiyuu?

Намайг хүлээж
байхгүй юу ?

I'll be back in ... minutes.
bi ... minutyn daraa
butsaad iren
(see page 146 for numbers)

Би ... минутын дараа
буцаад ирнэ.

How much do I owe you?
bi khedüig tölökh ve?

Би хэдийг төлөх вэ?

Directions
Turn left.
züün tiishee ereg

Зүүн тийшээ эргэ.

Turn right.
baruun tiishee ereg

Баруун тийшээ эргэ.

Go straight ahead.
deeshee chigeeree yav

Дээшээ чигээрээ яв.

Please slow down.
jaakhan udaan yavanuu?

Жаахан удаан явна уу?

Please hurry.
jaakhan khurdan yavanuu?

Жаахан хурдан явна уу?

Please stop here.
end zogsonuu   Энд зогсоно уу?
This is the wrong way.
en buruu zam   Энэ буруу зам.

Some Useful Words

above/at	*deer*	дээр
address	*khayag*	хаяг
around here	*en khaviar*	энэ хавиар
arrive	*irekh*	ирэх
below	*door*	доор
bicycle	*unadag dugui*	унадаг дугуй
bus stop	*avtobusny zogsool*	автобусны зогсоол
Careful!	*bolgoomjtoi!*	Болгоомжтой!
depart	*yavakh*	явах
early	*ert*	эрт
far	*khol*	хол
map	*gazryn zurag*	газрын зураг
motorbike	*mototsikl*	мотоцикл
near	*oir*	ойр
over there	*en khavid*	энэ хавьд
seat	*suudal*	суудал
Stop!	*zogs!*	Зогс!
ticket	*tasalbar/bilet*	тасалбар/билет
timetable	*tsagiin khuvaair*	цагийн хувaарь
Wait!	*khüleej bai!*	Хүлээж бай!

GETTING AROUND

Accommodation

The big hotels in Ulan Bator offer accommodation ranging from 'de luxe' (*büten lyuks*) and 'demi-luxe' (*khagas lyuks*) to standard (*engiin*), although one or two classify their rooms as 1st, 2nd or 3rd class. Some hotels charge a room rate, others charge per person, but in either case foreigners are expected to pay in dollars a great deal more than Mongols pay in *tögrög*. Reception staff at Ulan Bator hotels speak some English, but elsewhere you'll need Mongolian to negotiate your stay. The hotels in provincial centres may have seen better days, but they look like hotels and offer basic facilities, including central heating and hot water at certain times. They should accept *tögrög*. Accommodation in district centres is mostly limited to barrack-style huts (cubicles or open plan) for lorry drivers. In Gobi districts there may be no piped water supply. The lower you go down the scale the cheaper it gets. Take your own soap and toilet paper.

Finding Accommodation

Can you recommend a ... hotel?	... *neg zochid buudal zaaj ögökhgüi yüü?*	... нэг зочид буудал зааж өгөхгүй юу?
central	*khotyn tövd*	Хотын төвд
cheap	*khyamdkhan*	Хямдхан
good	*saikhan*	Сайхан
nearby	*oirkhon*	Ойрхон

Could you write down the
name and address for me,
please?

ta ner, khayagygen bichij
ögnüü?

Та нэр хаягыг нь бичиж
өгнө үү?

Can you show me on the
map?

ta nadad gazryn zurag
deer üzüülekhgüi yüü?

Та надад газрын зураг
дээр үзүүлэхгүй юу?

Can I walk there?

bi tiishee alkhaj ochij
bolokhuu?

Би тийшээ алхаж очиж
болох уу?

Yes, it's not far.

bolon khol bish

Болно, хол биш.

No, it's a long way.

bolokhgüi khol

Болохгүй, хол.

At the Hotel
Checking In

Do you have any rooms
available?

tanaid sul öröö bainuu?

Танайд сул өрөө байна уу?

Do you have a reservation?

ta uridchilan zakhialsanuu?

Та урьдчилан захиалсан уу?

Yes, here's the confirmation.

tiimee bichigen en bain

Тиймээ, бичиг нь энэ байна.

I would like ...	*bi ... avi*	Би ... авъя.
a single room	*neg khünii öröö*	нэг хүний өрөө
a double room	*khoyor khünii öröö*	хоёр хүний өрөө

a twin-bed room	*khoyor ortoi öröö*	хоёр ортой өрөө
a double-bed room	*khoyor khünii ortoi öröö*	хоёр хүний ортой өрөө
I want a room with a ...	*bi ... öröö avmaar bain*	Би ... өрөө авмаар байна.
bath	*ongotstoi/vanntai*	онгоцтой/ ваннатай
shower	*shürshüürtei*	шүршүүртэй
telephone	*utastai*	утастай
television	*televiztei*	телевизтэй
window	*tsonkhtoi*	цонхтой

How much does the room cost?

en öröö yamar üntei ve? Энэ өрөө ямар үнэтэй вэ?

What's the price per night/ week?

khonogt/doloo khonogt yamar üntei ve? Хоногт/долоо хоногт ямар үнэтэй вэ?

Can I see the room?

bi öröögöö üzej bolokhuu? Би өрөөгөө үзэж болох уу?

I don't like this room.

bi avakhaa boliloo Би авахаа болилоо.

Are there any others?

öör öröö bainuu? Өөр өрөө байна уу?

Are there any better ones?

arai saikhan öröö bainuu? Арай сайхан өрөө байна уу?

Are there any cheaper ones?

arai khyamdkhan öröö bainuu? Арай хямдхан өрөө байна уу?

It's fine, I'll take it.
saikhan öröö bain bi avi   Сайхан өрөө байна, би авъя.

I want to stay for ...	*bi ... khonomoor bain*	Би ... хономоор байна.
one night	*neg*	нэг
two nights	*khoyor*	хоёр
three nights	*gurav*	гурав
a week	*doloo*	долоо

Problems

It's too ...	*kheterkhii ... bain*	Хэтэрхий ... байна.
expensive	*üntei*	үнэтэй
hot	*khaluun*	халуун
cold	*khüiten*	хүйтэн
big	*tom*	том
small	*bag*	бага
dark	*kharankhui*	харанхуй
noisy	*shuugiantai*	шуугиантай
dirty	*bokhir*	бохир

I need some ...	*nadad ... kheregtei bain*	Надад ... хэрэгтэй байна.
soap	*savang*	саван
towels	*nüür garyn alchuur*	нүүр гарын алчуур
toilet paper	*jorlongiin tsaas*	жорлонгийн цаас
hot water	*khaluun us*	халуун ус
coat hangers	*khuvtsasny ölgüür*	хувцасны өлгүүр

The ... doesn't work.	*... ajillakhgüi bain*	... ажиллахгүй байна.

Can you repair the ...?	... *zasakhuu?*	... засах уу?
central heating	*negdsen khalaalt*	Нэгдсэн халаалт
light	*gerel*	Гэрэл
lock	*tsooj*	Цоож
shower	*shürshüür*	Шүршүүр
socket	*zalguuryn suuir*	Залгуурын суурь
tap (faucet)	*tsorog*	Цорго
toilet	*jorlong*	Жорлон

Some Useful Phrases

Your room is on the fifth floor.
  tany öröö tavdugaar davkhart baigaa Таны өрөө тавдугаар давхарт байгаа.

Number ...
  ... dugaar öröö ... дугаар өрөө.

My room number is ...
  minii öröönii dugaar ... Миний өрөөний дугаар ...
  (see the Numbers chapter)

Can I have my key please?
  minii tülkhüüriig ögööch? Миний түлхүүрийг өгөөч?

Do you have somewhere to store valuables?
  üntei yumaa tusgai khadgalamjind khadgaluulakhuu? Үнэтэй юмаа тусгай хадгаламжинд хадгалуулах уу?

Can you store this for me?
  üüniig nadad khadgalj ögnüü? Үүнийг надад хадгалж өгнө үү?

Has anybody left me a
message?
   nadad khün yum   Надад хүн юм
   khelüüleegüi yüü?   хэлүүлээгүй юү?
Where is the dining room?
   khoolny öröö khaan   Хоолны өрөө хаана
   bain ve?   байна вэ?
My room has not been
cleaned.
   minii öröög tseverleegüi   Миний өрөөг цэвэрлээгүй
   bain   байна.
Please change the sheets.
   tsagaan khereglel solikhuu?   Цагаан хэрэглэл солих уу?

Checking Out

We would like to	*bid öröögöö*	Бид өрөөгөө
check out ...	... *sullan*	... суллана.
now	*odoo*	одоо
at noon	*ödör dund*	өдөр дунд
tomorrow	*margaash*	маргааш

Can you get my bill ready (for
the morning)?
   minii tootsoog (öglöö)   Миний тооцоог (өглөө)
   belen bolgoj ögönüü?   бэлэн болгож өгнө үү?
Can I leave my bags in the
lobby?
   achaagaa üüdnii tankhimd   Ачаагаа үүдний танхимд
   orkhij bolokhuu?   орхиж болох уу?

| I'm returning ... | *bi ... butsan* | Би ... буцана. |
| tomorrow | *margaash* | маргааш |

| the day after tomorrow | *nögöödör* | нөгөөдөр |
| in a few days | *khed khonogiin daraa* | хэд хоногийн дараа |

Laundry

Could I have these clothes ...?	*en khuvtsasyg ... bolokh ve?*	Энэ хувцасыг ... болох уу?
washed	*ugaalgaj*	угаалгаж
ironed	*indüüdj*	индүүдж
dry-cleaned	*tseverlüülj*	цэвэрлүүлж

When will they be ready?
khezee belen bolokh ve?   Хэзээ бэлэн болох вэ?

I need it ...	*... kheregtei*	... хэрэгтэй.
today	*önöödör*	Өнөөдөр
tomorrow	*margaash*	Маргааш
the day after tomorrow	*nögöödör*	Нөгөөдөр

Is my laundry ready?
minii khuvtsas bolsonuu?   Миний хувцас болсон уу?

This isn't mine.
en miniikh bish   Энэ минийх биш.

There's a piece missing.
neg yum dutuu bain   Нэг юм дутуу байна.

Cash on delivery.
möngöö yumaa avakhdaa tushaagaarai!   Мөнгөө юмаа авахдаа тушаагаарай!

Some Useful Words

address	*khayag*	хаяг
bathroom	*ugaalgyn öröö*	угаалгын өрөө
bed	*or*	ор
bill	*tootsoo*	тооцоо
blanket	*khönjil*	хөнжил
bolt	*tügjee*	түгжээ
candle	*laa*	лаа
chair	*sandal*	сандал
clean	*tseverkhen*	цэвэрхэн
cot	*khüükhdiin or*	хүүхдийн ор
de luxe	*büten lyuks*	бүтэн люкс
demi-luxe	*khagas lyuks*	хагас люкс
dining room	*khoolny öröö*	хоолны өрөө
dirty	*bokhir*	бохир
double bed	*khoyor khünii or*	хоёр хүний ор
electricity	*tsakhilgaan*	цахилгаан
fan	*salkhin sens*	салхин сэнс
first class	*negdügeer zereg*	нэгдүгээр зэрэг
floor (storey)	*davkhar*	давхар
key	*tülkhüür*	түлхүүр
lift (elevator)	*lift*	лифт
light bulb	*gerliin shil*	гэрлийн шил
lock (n)	*tsooj*	цоож
mattress	*devsger/gudas*	дэвсгэр/гудас
mirror	*toil*	толь
pillow	*der*	дэр
quiet	*taivan*	тайван
receptionist	*zochid khüleen*	зочид хүлээн
	avagch	авагч
second class	*khoyordugaar zereg*	хоёрдугаар зэрэг

sheet	*orny tsagaan daavuu*	орны цагаан даавууоар
shower	*shürshüür*	шүршүүр
soap	*savang*	саван
standard	*engiin*	энгийн
suitcase	*chemdan*	чемодан
table	*shiree*	ширээ
third class	*guravdugaar zereg*	гуравдугаар зэрэг
toilet	*jorlong*	жорлон
toilet paper	*jorlongiin tsaas*	жорлонгийн цаас
towel	*nüür garyn alchuur*	нүүр гарын алчуур
washing powder	*ugaalgyn nuntag*	угаалгын нунтаг
window	*tsonkh*	цонх

Around Town

Very little of Mongolia's capital Ulan Bator is more than a hundred years old but besides modern museums and government buildings its landmarks include monasteries and temples containing rich collections of Buddhist art. The most important of these are the Bogd Khan's Winter Palace (*bogd khaany övliin ordon*, Богд хааны өвлийн ордон), the Religious History Museum (*shashny tüükhiin muzei*, Шашны түүхийн музей) at Choijin Lama Temple (*choijin lamyn süm*, Чойжин ламын сүм) and Gandan monastery (*gandan khiid,* Гандан хийд), the country's Buddhist centre. Most of central Ulan Bator, consisting of broad avenues of multistorey office and apartment blocks, was built in the past 30 years, but here and there you can discover old Russian-style houses. The State Palace (*töriin ordon*, Төрийн ордон) stands on the north side of the main Sükhbaatar Square (*sükhbaataryn talbai*, Сүхбаатарын талбай), and the opera and ballet theatre at the southeastern corner. Most places of interest are within walking distance of the main hotels.

I want to go to the ...	*bi ... ruu yavmaar bain*	Би ... руу явмаар байна.
Where is the nearest ...?	*oirkhon ... khaan bain ve?*	... ойрхон хаана байна вэ?
I am looking for the ...	*bi ... erj yavan*	Би ... эрж явна.

74

AROUND TOWN

Please show me the way to the ...	*ta ... zaaj ögönüü?*	Та ... зааж өгнө үү?
airport	*nisekh ongotsny buudlyg*	нисэх онгоцны буудлыг
art gallery	*dürslekh urlagyn muzeig*	дүрслэх урлагын музейг
bank	*bank*	банк
bus stop	*avtobusny zogsool*	автобусны зогсоол
(British) embassy	*(angliin) elchin yaamyg*	(Английйн) элчин яамыг
department store	*ikh delgüüriig*	их дэлгүүрийг
Hotel Bayangol	*Bayangol zochid buudlyg*	Баянгол зочид буудлыг
Hotel Ulaanbaatar	*Ulaanbaatar zochid buudlyg*	Улаанбаатар зочид буудлыг
Hotel Chinggis Khaan (Genghis Khan)	*Chingis Khaan zochid buudlyg*	Чингис Хаан зочид буудлыг
main square	*khotyn töv talbaig*	хотын төв талбайг
market	*zakhyg*	захыг
post office	*shuudangiin salbar*	шуудангийн салбар
railway station	*galt tergenii buudlyg*	галт тэрэгний буудлыг

When will it open?
khezee ongoikh ve?   Хэзээ онгойх вэ?
When will it close?
khezee khaakh ve?   Хэзээ хаах вэ?

At the Post Office

The biggest post office in Mongolia is just round the southwestern corner of Sükhbaatar Square in central Ulan Bator. You can buy stamps and postcards, send telegrams in the main hall and post parcels from there also. The side halls are waiting rooms for bookable long-distance phone calls. There are newspaper and book stalls in the lobby. The postal service in Mongolia delivers to numbered post office boxes, but in rural areas the nearest post office may be many miles away.

I'd like to send a ...	*bi ... yavuulmaar bain*	Би ... явуулмаар байна.
letter	*zakhidal*	захидал
postcard	*il zakhidal*	ил захидал
parcel	*ilgeemj*	илгээмж
telegram	*tsakhilgaan*	цахилгаан

I'd like to send this to ...	*bi üüniig ... ruu yavuulmaar bain*	Би үүнийг ... руу явуулмаар байна.
How much is it to send this to ...?	*üüniig ... ruu yavuulakhad ünen yamar baikhve?*	Үүнийг ... руу явуулахад үнэ нь ямар байх вэ?
Australia	*Avstrali Uls*	Австрали Улс
England	*Angil Uls*	Англи Улс
Hong Kong	*Gongkong*	Гонконг
Japan	*Yapon Uls*	Япон Улс
the USA	*Amerikiin Negdsen Uls*	Америкийн Нэгдсэн Улс

AROUND TOWN

Can you wrap this for me?
ta üüniig nadad booj ögch
chadakhuu?

Та үүнийг надад боож өгч чадах уу?

I would like to send a telegram.
bi tsakhilgaan yavuuli

Би цахилгаан явуулъя.

Here is the address.
khayagen en bain

Хаяг нь энэ байна.

How much per word?
neg üg yamar üntei ve?

Нэг үг ямар үнэтэй вэ?

Some Useful Words

by airmail	*agaaraar*	агаараар
envelope	*dugtui*	дугтуй
express	*yaaraltai*	яаралтай
letter	*zakhidal*	захидал
parcel	*ilgeemj*	илгээмж
post	*shuudang*	шуудан
post box	*shuudangiin*	шуудангийн
	khairtsag	хайрцаг
poste restante	*ööröö avakh*	өөрөө авах
(letter)	*(zakhidal)*	(захидал)
registered	*batalgaatai*	баталгаатай
stamp	*shuudangiin mark*	шуудангийн марк
by surface mail	*gazraar*	газраар

Telephone

Mongolia is only just beginning to realise that the phone is for communication and not just a status symbol. There are two parallel telephone systems, the old Soviet-style operator-managed system with about 60,000 numbers country-wide, and a modern international satellite autodialling system with a few hundred official and foreign subscribers in Ulan Bator. There are no person-to-person, collect (reverse charges) or charge-card calls for the moment. There are also no call boxes (payphones). If you can't persuade a local company or private subscriber to let you use the phone, you will have to make your call through the hotel switchboard or go to the local post office and order a timed call many hours in advance. The telephone network in the countryside is in a bad state because the equipment is very old, and the copper wires are often stolen by scrap metal dealers.

I would like to make a long-distance call to ...	
bi ... ruu kholyn duudlagaar yarimaar bain	Би ... руу холын дуудлагаар яримаар байна.
I would like to make a (... -minute) call to ...	
bi ... ruu yarikh (... minutiin) zakhialag ögmöör bain	Би ... руу ярих (... минутийн) захиалга өгмөөр байна.
The number is ...	
dugaar ...	Дугаар ...
How much will it cost?	
ünen yamar ve?	Үнэ нь ямар вэ?
There's no answer.	
khariu ögökhgüi bain	Хариу өгөхгүй байна.
You're through (ie connected)!	
odoo yariarai!	Одоо яриарай!
Have you finished?	
yairj duussanuu?	Ярьж дууссан уу?
Hello?	
bainuu?	Байна уу?

Who's calling?
  khen be?   Хэн вэ?
Do you speak English?
  ta angilaar yardaguu?   Та англиар ярьдаг уу?
I would like to speak to Mr
(Ganbold).
  bi (Ganbold) guaitai yarikh   Би (Ганболд) гуайтай ярих
  gesen yum   гэсэн юм.
He/She's not here.
  ter end baikhgüi bain   Тэр энд байхгүй байна.
Hang on a minute.
  khüleej baigaarai!   Хүлээж байгаарай!
Sorry, I got the wrong
number.
  örshöögöörei, bi buruu   Өршөөгөөрэй, би буруу
  ögchee   өгчээ.
I've been cut off!
  tasarchikhlaa!   Тасарчихлаа!

AROUND TOWN

Some Useful Words

telephone	*utas/telefon*	утас/телефон
telephone number	*utasny dugaar*	утасны дугаар
public telephone	*niitiin utas*	нийтийн утас
engaged	*utas yariad bain*	утас яриад байна
operator	*zalgagch*	залгагч
out of order	*gemteltei*	гэмтэлтэй

At the Bank

The 'bank' in this case means 'exchange facility', and changing
money and cashing travellers' cheques is much easier at Ulan
Bator's hotels than anywhere else, although you can change

money at exchange booths and even banks if you need to. You will be asked to show your passport and sign a receipt, and commission will be charged on the transaction. Although the Mongolian *tögrög* was floated on the free currency market in 1993, you may still be approached in the street to 'change money'. This is no longer strictly illegal, and the rate offered might be better than the official one, but you might be cheated, too. Everybody is interested in *nogoon* (greenbacks), and it would be useful to carry some US dollars in small notes for casual purchases. Avoid exchanging large sums into *tögrög* which you might later find difficult to spend.

I would like to change some money.
  bi möng solimoor bain   Би мөнгө солимоор байна.
I would like to change some travellers' cheques.
  bi juulchny chek solimoor bain   Би жуулчны чек солимоор байна.
What is the exchange rate?
  solikh jansh yamar bain?   Солих ханш ямар байна?
Please write it down for me.
  ta nadad bichij ögööch!   Та надад бичиж өгөөч!

I'd like to change some ...	*bi kheden ... solimoor bain*	Би хэдэн ... солимоор байна.
US$	*Amerikiin dollar*	Америкийн (АНУ-ын) доллар
UK£	*Ikh Britanii funt*	Их Британий фунт
Australian $	*Avstraliin dollar*	Австралийн доллар
Canadian $	*Kanadyn dollar*	Канадын доллар
Hong Kong $	*Gongkongiin dollar*	Гонконгийн доллар
Deutschmarks	*Germany mark*	Германы марк

Japanese yen	*Yapony yen*	Японы иен
Russian roubles	*Orosyn ruubl*	Оросын (ОХУ-ын) рубль
Chinese yuan	*Khyatadyn yuan*	Хятадын юань

Some Useful Words

bankdraft	*bankny chek*	банкны чек
banknote	*möngön temdegt*	мөнгөн тэмдэгт
cash	*belen möng*	бэлэн мөнгө
cashier	*kass*	касс
credit card	*kredit kard*	кредит кард
exchange desk	*möng solikh gazar*	мөнгө солих газар
small change	*zadgai möng*	задгай мөнгө
signature	*garyn üseg*	гарын үсэг
travellers' cheque	*juulchny chek*	жуулчны чек

Sightseeing

Excuse me, what's that ...?	*uuchlaarai, ter ... yuu ve?*	Уучлаарай, тэр ... юу вэ?
building	*baishing*	байшин
monument	*khöshöö*	хөшөө
park	*tsetserleg*	цэцэрлэг

Do you have a map/town map?
tanaid gazryn/khotyn zurag bainuu?
Танайд газрын/хотын зураг байна уу?

Can I take photographs?
bi zurag avch bolokhuu?
Би зураг авч болох уу?

Can I take your photograph?
bi tany zurgiig avch bolokhuu?
Би таны зургийг авч болох уу?

I'll send you the photos later.

bi tand daraa ʒurag yavuulan

Би танд дараа зураг явуулна.

Please write down your name and address.

ta ner, khayagaa bichij ögnüü?

Та нэр, хаягаа бичиж өгнө үү?

What time does it open?

kheden tsagt ongoidog ve?

Хэдэн цагт онгойдог вэ?

What time does it close?

kheden tsagt khaadag ve?

Хэдэн цагт хаадаг вэ?

Some Useful Words

art gallery	*dürslekh urlagiin muzei*	дүрслэх урлагийн музей
cemetery	*orshuulgyn gazar*	оршуулгын газар
exhibition	*üzesgelen*	үзэсгэлэн
housing	*oron suuts*	орон сууц
library	*nomyn sang*	номын сан
market	*zakh*	зах
monastery	*khiid*	хийд
museum	*muzei*	музей
palace	*ordon*	ордон
shop	*delgüür*	дэлгүүр
square	*talbai*	талбай
stadium	*tsengeldekh khüreelen*	цэнгэлдэх хүрээлэн
stock exchange	*khöröngiin birj*	хөрөнгийн бирж
street	*gudamj*	гудамж
temple	*süm*	сүм
theatre	*teatr*	театр
university	*ikh surguuil*	их сургууль

Signs

ОРЦ	ENTRANCE
ГАРЦ	EXIT
ОРЖ БОЛОХГҮЙ	NO ENTRANCE
ГАРЧ БОЛОХГҮЙ	NO EXIT
ЭМЭГТЭЙН	LADIES
ЭРЭГТЭЙН	GENTLEMEN
ТАТ	PULL
ТҮЛХ	PUSH
ХАДГАЛСАН	RESERVED/ENGAGED
ХООСОН	VACANT
ЕРӨНХИЙ ЖИЖҮҮР	RECEPTION
КАСС	CASHIER
ЛАВЛАГАА	INFORMATION
ШУУДАН	POST
ТАКСИ	TAXI
ХААСАН	CLOSED
СУУДАЛГҮЙ	SOLD OUT
БОЛГООМЖИЛ	CAUTION
ЗАСВАРТАЙ	UNDER REPAIR
ТАМХИ ТАТАЖ БОЛОХГҮЙ	NO SMOKING
ЗУРАГ АВЧ БОЛОХГҮЙ	NO PHOTOGRAPHY

AROUND TOWN

Nightlife

Hotel discos provide the usual attractions of loud pop music and alcohol. The opera, theatre and cinemas finish early, but some of Ulan Bator's new restaurants and 'nightclubs' advertise live music, karaoke and strip shows. Sex has also been privatised.

AROUND TOWN

What's there to do in the
evenings?
   oroi yuu khiikh ve?   Орой юу хийх вэ?
Is there a disco here?
   end disko bainuu?   Энд диско байна уу?
Can I buy a tape of this
music?
   bi en khögjmiin khuurtsgyg   Би энэ хөгжмийн хуурцагыг
   avch bolokhuu?   авч болох уу?

I'd like to see ...	*bi ... üzmeer bain*	Би ... үзмээр байна.
the circus	*tsirk*	цирк
a horsehead fiddle	*morin khuur*	морин хуур
a movie	*kino*	кино
an opera	*duuir*	дуурь
overtone singing	*khöömii*	хөөмий
a play	*jüjig*	жүжиг
a song and dance troupe	*duu büjgiin chuulag*	дуу бүжгийн чуулга
traditional wrestling	*mongol bökh*	монгол бөх

I'd like two tickets	*bi ... bilet*	Би ... билет
for the show ...	*khoyoryg avi*	хоёрыг авъя!
this evening	*önöö oroin*	өнөө оройн
tomorrow evening	*margaash oroin*	маргааш оройн

AROUND TOWN

Some Useful Words

ballet	*büjgiin jüjig*	бүжгийн жүжиг
ballroom dancing	*niitiin büjig*	нийтийн бүжиг
cinema	*kinoteatr*	кинотеатр
concert	*kontsert*	концерт
disco	*disko*	диско
folksong	*ardyn duu*	ардын дуу
jazz	*djaz*	джаз
opera	*duuir*	дуурь

In the Country

From the forests and snowcapped mountains of the north and west to the sand-dunes of the south and the wild flowers of the rolling eastern steppe, the natural beauty and variety of the Mongolian countryside are made all the more memorable by the remarkable people who live there. Mongolia is one of the few places on earth where the nomadic lifestyle is still practised, and no visit is complete without watching herdsmen at work with their animals. To experience nomad hospitality, when you spot a *ger* during a cross-country journey or sightseeing trip simply drive over and call in (see Greetings & Civilities chapter).

Some Useful Phrases

Where is the driver?
   jolooch khaan bain ve?   Жолооч хаана байна вэ?
Where have you been?
   khaanaas irev?   Хаанаас ирэв?
Where are we going?
   khaashaa yavakh ve?   Хаашаа явах вэ?
How many kilometres is it?
   zamyn urt kheden   Замын урт хэдэн
   kilometr ve?   километр вэ?
When do we leave?
   bid kheden tsagt yavakh ve?   Бид хэдэн цагт явах вэ?

To the ...

north	*khoid züg*	Хойд зүг.
south	*ömön züg*	Өмнө зүг.
east	*züün züg*	Зүүн зүг.
west	*baruun züg*	Баруун зүг.
provincial capital	*aimgiin töv rüü*	Аймгийн төв рүү.
district centre	*sumyn töv rüü*	Сумын төв рүү.

IN THE COUNTRY

The Herder's Home

We would like to see inside a herder's yurt (felt tent).

bid malchny gert orj üzmeer bain

Бид малчны гэрт орж үзмээр байна.

How long will it take to get there?

tend khürekhed ailkher udakh ve?

Тэнд хүрэхэд аль хэр удах вэ?

Can we walk?
bid yavgan yavj bolokhuu?   Бид явган явж болох уу?
Call off the dogs!
nokhoigoo!   Нохойгоо!
We would like to drink some koumiss.
bid airag umaar bain   Бид айраг умаар байна.

cooking pot	*togoo*	тогоо
cowdung box	*argalyn avdar*	аргалын авдар
door	*khaalag*	хаалга
felt material	*esgii*	эсгий
felt roof cover	*deever*	дээвэр
koumiss bag	*khökhüür*	хөхүүр
skylight	*toon*	тооно
skylight cover	*örkh*	өрх
stove	*zuukh*	зуух
support post	*bagan*	багана
wall section	*khan*	хана
yurt	*ger*	гэр

Livestock Raising

camel	*temee*	тэмээ
chicken	*takhia*	тахиа
cow	*ünee*	үнээ
donkey	*iljig*	илжиг
enclosure	*malyn khashaa*	малын хашаа
goat	*yamaa*	ямаа
herding	*mal aj akhui*	мал аж ахуй
horse	*moir*	морь
pig	*gakhai*	гахай
poultry farm	*shuvuuny aj akhui*	шувууны аж ахуй

IN THE COUNTRY

summer camp	*zuslang*	зуслан
yak	*sarlag*	сарлаг

I'd like to ride a ...	*bi ... yavakh gesen yum*	Би ... явах гэсэн юм.
horse	*morior*	мориор
camel	*temeegeer*	тэмээгээр
yak	*sarlagaar*	сарлагаар

bridle	*khazaar*	хазаар
hitching line	*uyaa*	уяа
hobble	*chödör*	чөдөр
lasso pole	*uurag*	уурга
saddle	*emeel*	эмээл
stirrup	*döröö*	дөрөө
whip	*tashuur*	ташуур

Crop Farming

agriculture	*khödöö aj akhui*	хөдөө аж ахуй
arable land	*tarialang*	тариалан
barley	*arvai*	арвай
cabbage	*baitsaa*	байцаа
combine harvester	*kombain*	комбайн
fodder	*tejeel*	тэжээл
fruit	*jims*	жимс
grass/hay	*övs*	өвс
maize	*erden shish*	эрдэнэ шиш
melon	*amtat gua*	амтат гуа
oats	*ovyoos*	овъёос
onion	*songin*	сонгино
plough	*anjis*	анжис

potatoes	*töms*	төмс
sunflower	*naran tsetseg*	наран цэцэг
tractor	*traktor*	трактор
vegetable	*nogoo*	ногоо
wheat	*buudai*	буудай

Weather

What's the weather like?
   tenger yamar bain?   Тэнгэр ямар байна?

It's cold.	*khüiten bain*	Хүйтэн байна.
It's hot.	*khaluun bain*	Халуун байна.
It's raining.	*boroo orj bain*	Бороо орж байна.
It's snowing.	*tsas orj bain*	Цас орж байна.
It's windy.	*salkhtai bain*	Салхитай байна.

The weather is nice today.
   önöödör tenger saikhan   Өнөөдөр тэнгэр сайхан
   bain   байна.
Will it rain tomorrow?
   margaash boroo orokhuu? Маргааш бороо орох уу?
Will it be cold?
   khüitrekhüü?   Хүйтрэх үү?

IN THE COUNTRY

cloud	*üül*	үүл
dust	*toos*	тоос
frost	*tsang*	цан
ice	*mös*	мөс
mud	*shavar*	шавар
rain	*boroo*	бороо
snow	*tsas*	цас
soil	*khörs*	хөрс
sunny	*nartai*	нартай
weather forecast	*tsag uuriin medee*	цаг уурын мэдээ
wind	*salikh*	салхи

Seasons

spring	*khavar*	хавар
summer	*zun*	зун
autumn	*namar*	намар
winter	*övöl*	өвөл

Some Useful Words

cave	*agui*	агуй
coniferous forest	*taiga*	тайга
countryside	*khödöö*	хөдөө
desert	*tsöl*	цөл
earthquake	*gazar khödlöl*	газар хөдлөл
flood	*üyer*	үер
Gobi	*goiv*	говь
plain	*kheer tal*	хээр тал
hill	*dov*	дов
hot spring	*khaluun rashaan*	халуун рашаан
lake	*nuur*	нуур
marsh	*namag*	намаг

monastery	*khiid*	хийд
mountain	*uul*	уул
mountain pass	*davaa*	даваа
mountain range	*nuruu*	нуруу
nature reserve	*darkhan gazar*	дархан газар
river	*gol/mörön*	гол/мөрөн
saltmarsh	*khujir*	хужир
spring	*bulag*	булаг
temple	*süm*	сүм
town	*khot*	хот
valley	*khöndii*	хөндий
village	*tosgon*	тосгон
waterfall	*khürkhree*	хүрхрээ
well	*khudag*	худаг
woods/forest	*oi*	ой

Trees & Wild Plants

birch	*khus*	хус
buckthorn	*chatsargan*	чацаргана
caragana bush	*khargan*	харгана
edelweiss	*tsagaan türüü*	цагаан түрүү
feather grass	*khyalgan*	хялгана
fir	*gatsuur*	гацуур
juniper	*arts*	арц
larch	*khargai/khar mod*	харгай/хар мод
mushroom	*möög*	мөөг
nettle	*khalgai*	халгай
pine	*nars*	нарс
rhubarb	*gishüün*	гишүүнэ
saxaul bush	*zag*	заг
tumble weed	*khamkhuul*	хамхуул
willow	*burgas*	бургас

Animals & Birds

bear	*baavgai*	баавгай
bird	*shuvuu*	шувуу
cat	*muur*	муур
deer/reindeer	*bug*	буга
dog	*nokhoi*	нохой
duck	*nugas*	нугас
eagle	*bürged*	бүргэд

fish	*zagas*	загас
frog	*melkhii*	мэлхий
gazelle	*zeer*	зээр
goose	*galuu*	галуу
lammergeier	*yol*	ёл
lizard	*gürvel*	гүрвэл
marmot	*tarvag*	тарвага
mountain goat	*yangir*	янгир

wild animal	*zerleg amitad*	зэрлэг амьтад
wild (Przewalski) horse	*takhi*	тахь
wild sheep	*argail*	аргаль
wolf	*chon*	чоно

Insects

ant	*shorgoolj*	шоргоолж
bee	*zögii*	зөгий
beetle	*tsokh*	цох
butterfly	*erveekhei*	эрвээхэй
cockroach	*joom*	жоом
fly	*yalaa*	ялаа
grasshopper	*tsartsaa*	царцаа
insect	*shaivj*	шавьж
mosquito	*shumuul*	шумуул
scorpion	*khilentset khorkhoi*	хилэнцэт хорхой
spider	*aalz*	аалз
tick	*khachig*	хачиг
wasp	*morin zögii*	морин зөгий

Food

Mongolian food is quite different from European or Chinese food. The cuisine is basically of four different kinds – rural (nomadic), rural (hunting), urban (national) and urban (international). There are considerable differences in the ingredients and methods of preparation.

Traditional methods witnessed by European travellers in the Mongol Empire over 600 years ago are still practised by Mongols living in the countryside today. On the other hand, Russian influence and industrial development in the 20th century have included manufactured foods like bread, macaroni and sugar in the diet of town-dwellers.

Tourists on package holidays used to have little or no exposure to real Mongolian food but were fed hotel meals consisting largely of fried eggs, skinny chicken-legs, beefburgers and chips fried in mutton fat. There was even a joke that, like the official communist literature of the time, the food was 'national in form but socialist in content'. Nowadays visitors have freedom of movement and choice and can explore a range of options in Ulan Bator's new restaurants or even in Mongolian homes in town and country. In the last few years authentic Chinese restaurants have begun to appear in Ulan Bator.

I'm hungry.
  bi ölsch bain   Би өлсч байна.
I'm thirsty.
  bi undaasch bain   Би ундаасч байна.
I'd like something to eat/
drink.
  bi yum idmeer/uumaar   Би юм идмээр/уумаар
  bain   байна.

Traditional Food

During the summer months Mongolian nomads mostly eat home-
made dairy products like cheeses and creams called 'white food'
or *tsagaan idee* (цагаан идээ), and drink koumiss (fermented
mare's milk), which they call *airag* (айраг). In the winter they
eat a lot of fatty meat, mostly mutton. Visitors are bound to be
drawn into Mongolian ritual when they eat traditional food in a
ger, which is the centre of the Mongol's microworld. Domestic
life turns about the stove, which stands at the centre of the *ger*
(see the Greetings & Civilities chapter). According to the rules of
Mongolian hospitality, visitors are offered refreshment any time
they call, and except in deserted regions Mongolian travellers
need not carry their own food.

Nomad's Delight

After visitors have been seated and the ritual exchange of questions and answers has moved on to more specific topics (see Greetings and Civilities), snuff bottles and cigarettes are passed round
while the woman of the *ger* pours a tea-based milky drink called
süütei tsai from a wooden jug into individual drinking bowls.
The tea is scraped from a solid pressed brick and boiled on the
stove in an iron cooking pot together with milk and other

ingredients according to taste – salt, butter, mutton fat or fried flour.

A bowl placed on a low table beside the stove contains a range of dried and unsalted high-fat cheeses and dried creams and hard pastries for nibbling or dunking. It is quite usual to be offered several different drinks one after the other, vodka and koumiss as well as tea.

Pieces of unsalted mutton are boiled lightly (to preserve the goodness) and then served from a communal bowl. The pieces are taken in the hands and strips of meat cut off the bone with a knife directly into the mouth. Cut towards yourself, and avoid turning the blade or point towards the host.

On special occasions a whole sheep is served, the shoulders on either side and the saddle (*uuts*) on top, surmounted by the head. The chief guest is invited to carve. The fatty tail (*khoniny süül*) is a particular delicacy amongst the Mongols. Another favourite is called 'four ribs' (*dörvön öndör*). You will see strips of air-dried meat (*borts*) hanging from the *ger* roof-poles.

When a sheep is slaughtered (it is killed by making a small incision near the heart and pinching an artery) the blood is collected for making sausages (*zaidas*).

Onion and garlic may be added to meat soups, but in the countryside you should not expect to be given any other vegetables or bread.

Dairy Produce

Except for the mares' milk reserved for making koumiss, milk is boiled and used for making various dried creams, curds, cheeses and butter, or dried or frozen for storage. Butter is made only from cow's, sheep's and goat's milk:

butter	*tsötsgiin tos*	цөцгийн тос
clarified butter	*shar tos*	шар тос
cheese	*byaslag*	бяслаг
cream	*tsötsgii*	цөцгий
sliced dried cream	*öröm*	өрөм
dried curd pieces	*aaruul*	ааруул
koumiss	*airag*	айраг
milk	*süü*	сүү
white food	*tsagaan idee*	цагаан идээ
sour cream	*tarag*	тараг
sour milk curds	*aarts*	аарц

Townspeople eating imported butter tend to call it *maasal* from the Russian word масло.

Traditional Dishes

FOOD

Flour used to be home-made from wild cereals but wheat flour was introduced by Russian settlers. Now factory-milled flour is generally available. The various kinds of tasty meat dumplings made all over Mongolia perhaps originated in China. They are very popular and can be bought from street stalls in Ulan Bator. The *bansh* dumplings are also used in soups:

deep-fried pastry	*boov*	боов
steamed bread	*mantuu*	мантуу
steamed meat dumpling	*buuz*	бууз
fried meat dumpling	*huushuur*	хуушуур
boiled meat dumpling	*bansh*	банш

Hunter's Choice

The main distinction between nomads' food and hunters' food is
that the former is prepared by women and boiled while the latter
is prepared by men and roasted or barbecued. The most famous
hunters' food is called *boodog*: the innards and bones of a whole
goat or marmot are removed through the neck and the carcass is
stuffed with hot stones taken with tongs from the campfire. A
little water is added and the carcass placed in the fire to roast.
Some nomads consider this to be wasteful, because cooking de-
stroys the animal's skin and fur. Hot stones from the fire are also
used to make *khorkhog*: chopped pieces of skinned lamb, marmot or kid and the hot stones are placed in alternate layers with a
little water in a small cooking pot which is sealed and shaken
regularly for half an hour or so. All kinds of game, deer, lope,
boar, duck, etc are hunted:

duck	*nugas*	нугас
goat	*yamaa*	ямаа
marmot	*tarvag*	тарвага
Mongolian antelope	*tsagaan zeer*	цагаан зээр
antevenison	*bugyn makh*	бугын мах
wild boar	*bodon gakhai*	бодон гахай

FOOD

Fish

Herdsmen don't eat fish (*zagas*, загас) but people living near the big lakes and rivers of northern Mongolia certainly do, and a fish barbecue is not to be missed. The products of Mongolia's small-scale fishing industry are also served occasionally in hotels and restaurants. If you're lucky you may be offered delicious varieties of Siberian salmon like *omul* (омуль) or *tul* (тул) – also called by its Russian name *taimen* (таймень) – or Siberian sturgeon (*khilem*, хилэм). Perch (*algan*, алгана) and pike (*tsurhkai*, цурхай) are caught in central Mongolia and carp (*buluu tsagaan*, булуу цагаан) in Lake Buir, eastern Mongolia.

Wild Berries

During the summer Mongolians visiting or living in the country-side pick wild berries to flavour various milk-based foods and drinks, the surplus being dried for winter use:

blackcurrant	*ükhriin nüd*	үхрийн нүд
blueberry	*ners*	нэрс
buckthorn	*chatsargan*	чацаргана
cranberry	*alirs*	алирс
redcurrant	*ulaalzgan*	улаалзгана
strawberry	*güzeelzgen*	гүзээлзгэнэ

FOOD

Modern Food

Mongolian townspeople tend to mix traditional and manufactured foods, buying meat and vegetables in the market and groceries in the local shops. These offer a range of locally produced preserves in jars and imported packaged and canned foodstuffs. While output of local products has declined in the past few years, more and more foreign goods have appeared on the previously almost empty shelves, including canned vegetables, chocolate bars, soft drinks, beers and spirits.

chocolate	*shokolad*	шоколад
coffee	*kofi*	кофе
flour	*guril*	гурил
fruit preserve	*nööshilsön jims*	нөөшилсөн жимс
honey	*zögiin bal*	зөгийн бал
macaroni	*khöndiin goimon*	хөндий гоймон
salt	*davs*	давс
sprats (canned)	*shproti/khar khaigan*	шпроты/хар хайган
sugar	*chikher*	чихэр
sweets	*tsaastai chikher*	цаастай чихэр
tea	*tsai*	цай
vegetable preserve	*nööshilsön nogoo*	нөөшилсөн ногоо

Breakfast

Cornflakes are expensive and have not caught on yet, and in any case milk has not been plentiful in the towns. For breakfast Mongolians mostly eat bread, egg or salami and drink tea, perhaps thickened with rice or flour into a kind of soup. A 'sandwich' is an open sandwich, not two slices of bread with a filling:

FOOD

breakfast	*öglöönii khool/tsai*	өглөөний хоол/цай
bread	*talkh*	талх
cheese	*byaslag*	бяслаг
cheese sandwich	*byaslagtai talkh*	бяслагтай талх
boiled egg	*chanasan öndög*	чанасан өндөг
fried egg	*sharsan öndög*	шарсан өндөг
jam	*jimsnii chanamal*	жимсний чанамал
omelette	*öndgön javrai*	өндгөн жаврай
sandwich	*buterbrod*	бутерброд
sausage	*khiam*	хиам
sausage sandwich	*khiamtai talkh*	хиамтай талх
toast	*khairsan talkh*	хайрсан талх

Hotel Fare

Ulan Bator's main hotel restaurants offer a range of European dishes including à la carte. The dining rooms at the tourist camps have fixed 'international' menus. Small hotels in the provinces serve only traditional food. No great distinction is made between lunch and dinner menus:

restaurant	*restoran*	ресторан
canteen	*guanz*	гуанз
tea shop	*tsainy gazar*	цайны газар
dining room	*zoogiin gazar*	зоогийн газар
lunch	*üdiin khool*	үдийн хоол
dinner	*oroin khool*	оройн хоол
menu	*khoolny tses*	хоолны цэс
à la carte	*zakhialag khool*	захиалга хоол
set dish	*belen khool*	бэлэн хоол

FOOD

first course	*negdügeer khool*	нэгдүгээр хоол
hors d'oeuvres (cold)	*khüiten zuush*	хүйтэн зууш
soup	*shöl*	шөл
second course	*khoyordugaar khool*	хоёрдугаар хоол
third course	*guravdugaar khool*	гуравдугаар хоол
dessert	*amtat zuush*	амтат зууш
cold	*khüiten*	хүйтэн
hot	*khaluun*	халуун

At the Restaurant

Waiter!
> *zöögchöö/üilchlegchee!*   Зөөгч өө!/Үйлчлэгч ээ!

Shall we sit there?
> *tend suukhuu?*   Тэнд суух уу?

Is this seat/are these seats taken?
> *khüntei yüü?*   Хүнтэй юу?

Show me the menu, please.
> *khoolny tsesee üzüülenüü?*   Хоолны цэсээ үзүүлнэ үү?

What have you got for lunch today?
> *tanaid önöödriin üdiin khoolond yuu yuu baindaa?*   Танайд өнөөдрийн үдийн хоолонд юу юу байна даа?

Isn't there any fish?
> *zagas baikhgüiyüü?*   Загас байхгүй юу?

I would like to have this.
> *bi en khoolyg avi!*   Би энэ хоолыг авъя!

Is this dish available?
> *en khool bainuu?*   Энэ хоол байна уу?

FOOD

It's finished (off).
  duuschikhsan!   Дуусчихсан!

More (another one), please!
  dakhiad khiinüü!   Дахиад хийнэ үү!

This is not what I ordered.
  en minii zakhialsan khool   Энэ миний захиалсан хоол
  bish!   биш!

Give me the same!
  önöökhiigöö ail!   Өнөөхийгөө аль!

The bill, please.
  tootsoogoo boduuli!   Тооцоогоо бодуулъя!

Soup

clear soup	*tungalag shöl*	тунгалаг шөл
thick soup	*zutan shöl*	зутан шөл
dumpling soup	*banshtai shöl*	банштай шөл
meat soup	*makhtai shöl*	махтай шөл
noodle soup	*guriltai shöl*	гурилтай шөл
vegetable soup	*nogootoi shöl*	ногоотой шөл

Meat

Pigs can't be herded, so Mongolian nomads don't eat pork, but there's no religious or other ban and it is readily available in town markets and restaurants:

beef	*ükhriin makh*	үхрийн мах
chicken	*takhiany makh*	тахианы мах
meat	*makh*	мах
mutton	*khoniny makh*	хонины мах
pork	*gakhain makh*	гахайн мах

FOOD

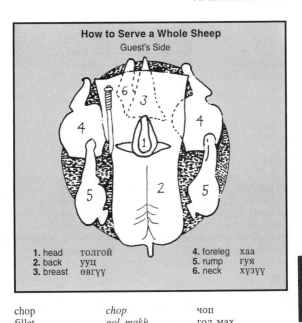

How to Serve a Whole Sheep
Guest's Side

1. head толгой	**4.** foreleg xaa
2. back ууц	**5.** rump гуя
3. breast өвгүү	**6.** neck хүзүү

FOOD

chop	*chop*	чоп
fillet	*gol makh*	гол мах
beefburger	*bifshteks*	бифштекс
(sometimes served with a fried egg on top)		
heart	*zürkh*	зүрх
kebab	*shorlog*	шорлог
liver	*eleg*	элэг
schnitzel	*shnitseil*	шницель
tongue	*khel*	хэл

Cooking & Preserving

boiled	*ch**a**nasan*	чанасан
fried	*sh**a**rsan*	шарсан
grilled/toasted	*kh**ai**rsan*	хайрсан
mashed	*n**u**khsan*	нухсан
roasted	*kh**uu**rsan*	хуурсан
steamed	*j**i**gnesen*	жигнэсэн
dried	*khat**aa**san*	хатаасан
frozen	*khöld**üü***	хөлдүү
preserved	***nöö**shilsön*	нөөшилсөн
salted	*d**a**vsalsan*	давсалсан
pickled	*d**a**rsan*	дарсан

Vegetables

Cultivated vegetables and cereals like millet and barley were introduced into Mongolia from the 17th century during the Qing (Manchu) period, when the importing of rice also began. Tomatoes and cucumber are available during the summer, but don't be surprised if for vegetables you are served both potatoes and rice, plus a spoonful of preserved cabbage:

cabbage	*b**ai**tsaa*	байцаа
carrot	*shar l**uu**van*	шар лууван
cucumber	***ö**rgöst kh**e**mekh*	өргөст хэмэх
onion	*s**o**ngin*	сонгино
potato	*töms*	төмс
radish	*ul**aa**n l**uu**van*	улаан лууван
rice	*tsag**aa**n bud**aa***	цагаан будаа
salad	*nog**oo**n zuush*	ногоон зууш
tomato	*ul**aa**n l**oo**il*	улаан лооль
turnip	*m**a**njin*	манжин
vegetable	*nog**oo***	ногоо

Mushrooms (*möög*) and wild rhubarb (*gishüün*) are picked and dried for medicinal rather than culinary purposes.

Vegetarian
Mongolia is tough on vegetarians (*nogoon khoolton*). If you really can't eat meat or animal fat, and you are unable to buy and cook your own vegetables, you'll need to bring your own supplies.

Desserts & Fruit

apple	*alim*	алим
banana	*gadil*	гадил
cake	*byaluu*	бялуу
dessert	*amtat zuush*	амтат зууш
fruit	*jims*	жимс
icecream	*zairmag/*	зайрмаг/
	mökhööldös	мөхөөлдөс
stewed fruit	*kompot*	компот
sweet melon	*amtat gua*	амтат гуа
water melon	*tarvas*	тарвас

Condiments & Flavourings

garlic	*sarmis*	сармис
ginger	*tsagaan gaa*	цагаан гаа
mustard	*gich*	гич
pepper	*povaair*	поваарь
salt	*davs*	давс
sugar	*chikher*	чихэр
vinegar	*tsuu*	цуу
vanilla	*vaniil*	ваниль

Drinks

The making of koumiss (fermented mares' milk), the nomad's summer drink, was first recorded amongst Scythian tribes nearly 2,500 years ago by the Greek historian Herodotus. The word koumiss (*qimiz*) is of Turkic origin, its Mongol name is *airag*.

Koumiss is fermented with a 'starter' from a previous batch in a cowskin bag holding some 200 litres and is ready to drink in three to five days – the higher the fat content, the longer it takes. The normal alcohol content of 3% may be increased by adding buckthorn berries, juniper, tea, etc. As a symbol of 'whiteness' and good fortune koumiss has a number of ceremonial uses.

Mongolian milk vodka (*arikh*) is distilled from cow's milk after the cream has been removed; its basic strength is 9% to 11%, but further distillations concentrate the alcohol.

Alcoholic Drinks

Mongolia distills wheat vodka (also called *arikh*) under various brand names, including 'Genghis Khan' and 'President Ochirbat'. Beer is called 'yellow koumiss' (*shar airag*) or *piv* (a Russian word). Hotel bars stock foreign beers and spirits.

bar	*baar*	баар
beer	*piv/shar airag*	пиво/шар айраг
koumiss	*airag*	айраг
vodka	*arikh*	архи
wine	*dars*	дарс

I'd like another bottle of beer please.

> *bi dakhiad neg shil shar airag avmaar bain*

Би дахиад нэг шил шар айраг авмаар байна.

CHINGGIS KHAN

70 CL 40%

MONGOLIAN VODKA

IMPORTED FROM THE MONGOLIAN PEOPLE'S REPUBLIC

No more vodka, thank you!
   arikh odoo bolon shüü!   Архи одоо болно шүү!
Cheers!
   erüül mendiin tölöö!   Эрүүл мэндийн төлөө!
I'm a teetotaler.
   bi arikh ogt uudaggüi   Би архи огт уудаггүй.

Non-Alcoholic Drinks

buckthorn juice	*chatsargany shüüs*	чацарганы шүүс
lemonade	*nimbegnii undaa*	нимбэгний ундаа
mineral water	*rashaan us*	рашаан ус
orange juice	*jürjiin shüüs*	жүржийн шүүс
black tea	*khar tsai*	хар цай
tea-based milky drink	*süütei tsai*	сүүтэй цай
coffee	*kofi*	кофе
cold water	*khüiten us*	хүйтэн ус
boiled water	*butsalgasan us*	буцалгасан ус

FOOD

Some Useful Words

Chopsticks (*savkh*) were introduced into Mongolia during the Qing (Manchu) period, but in this century they have been displaced everywhere by forks and spoons:

ashtray	*ünsnii sav*	үнсний сав
bottle	*shil*	шил
bowl/cup	*ayag*	аяга
burnt	*tülenkhii*	түлэнхий
cook (n)	*togooch*	тогооч
cook (v)	*khool khiikh*	хоол хийх
cooking pot	*togoo*	тогоо
fork	*seree*	сэрээ
gents'	*er khünii jorlong*	эр хүний жорлон
glass	*shilen ayag*	шилэн аяга
knife	*khutag*	хутга
ladies'	*em khünii jorlong*	эм хүний жорлон
napkin	*amny alchuur*	амны алчуур
plate	*tavag*	таваг
spoon	*khalbag*	халбага
table	*shiree*	ширээ
tough	*khatuu*	хатуу
wine glass	*khundag*	хундага

FOOD

Shopping

The 'flagship' of the capital's retail trade is the multistorey department store (*ikh delgüür*, Их дэлгүүр), which stands on Peace Avenue (*enkh taivny gudamj*, Энх тайвны гудамж) a few hundred yards west of the central post office at the corner of Sükhbaatar Square. Ulan Bator's 'big shop', which is what its name means, has been refurbished since the launching of the market economy and privatisation, and the various departments sell crockery, bicycles, stationery, ready-made clothing, etc. Western visitors are likely to find the range of goods narrow and the service slow – the 'consumer revolution' hasn't reached Mongolia yet.

Shops in Ulan Bator, even food shops, are few and far between. The biggest self-service store sells packaged foodstuffs, but you may have to queue for a shopping basket. Some of the small shops are converted ground-floor flats. While privatisation encouraged a lot of people to sink their savings into retail trade, most had too little capital to buy in much stock. They offer a small selection of imported shampoos, tights, toothpaste and poor-quality children's clothing. Many importers have no showrooms and advertise their Japanese TV sets, videos, cassette decks, refrigerators, etc and telephone numbers in the local press. A few art books or maps in foreign languages may be found in the bookshops, but dictionaries are hard to find. In country towns goods in the general stores are few and of poor quality. Most village shops stock only candles, matches, cooking pots and other odds and ends for herdsmen.

Ulan Bator's street stalls and central market offer a more colourful range of goods, including clothing, bloody joints of meat,

111

sacks of potatoes, green vegetables and fruit in season, fast foods like hot steamed meat dumplings (*buuz,* бууз), sponge cakes with green and pink icing, soft drinks and icecream. Cobblers mend shoes and handbags on the street, and newspapers and even single cigarettes are sold at bus stops.

Are there any shops near here?
en havdoir delgüür bainuu?   Энэ хавьд ойр дэлгүүр байна уу?

Will you show me the way to the shops?
ta delgüür zaaj ögnüü?   Та дэлгүүр зааж өгнө үү?

Where is the department store?
ikh delgüür khaan bain ve?   Их дэлгүүр хаана байна вэ?

Where is the ...?	... khaan bain?	... хаана байна?
baker's	talkhny delgüür	Талхны дэлгүүр
bank	bank	Банк
bookshop	nomyn delgüür	Номын дэлгүүр
clothes shop	khuvtsasny delgüür	Хувцасны дэлгүүр
confectioner's	nariin boovny delgüür	Нарийн боовны дэлгүүр
department store	ikh delgüür	Их дэлгүүр
dry cleaner's	khimi tseverlegeenii gazar	Хими цэвэрлэгээний газар

flower shop	tsetsgiin delgüür	Цэцгийн дэлгүүр
greengrocer's	jims nogoony delgüür	Жимс ногооны дэлгүүр
grocer's	khünsnii delgüür	Хүнсний дэлгүүр
laundry	ugaalgyn gazar	Угаалгын газар
market	zakh	Зах
pharmacy	emiin sang	Эмийн сан
shoe shop	gutlyn delgüür	Гутлын дэлгүүр
souvenir stall	beleg dursgalyn mukhlag	Бэлэг дурсгалын мухлаг
stationer's	bichgiin kheregleliin delgüür	Бичгийн хэрэглэлийн дэлгүүр
tailor's	zakhialag khuvtsasny delgüür	Захиалга хувцасны дэлгүүр

I'd like to buy ...
  bi ... avmaar bain   Би ... авмаар байна.
I'm just looking.
  bi yum üzej bain   Би юм үзэж байна.
How much does this cost?
  en yamar üntei ve?   Энэ ямар үнэтэй вэ?
That's very expensive!
  yaasan üntei yum be!   Яасан үнэтэй юм бэ!

Service

The onset of privatisation has sharpened up ideas about service.
At the 'big shop' things may still be rather slow and bureaucratic,
with separate queues to buy, pay and collect, but in the smaller
shops the motivation of ownership, however modest, encourages
shopkeepers and sales staff to be polite and even attentive. In the
big stores most goods will have fixed price tags, but in smaller

shops and on the street you should always try your luck at bargaining. Most Mongolian shopkeepers have only very vague ideas about foreign money and the relative value of their goods. If you don't want to pay their prices, they will most likely simply lose interest and return to their cigarette or newspaper, or the friend who dropped by for a chat.

Shop assistant!
   khudaldagchaa!   Худалдагч аа!
Come here, please.
   ta naash ir!   Та нааш ир!
Please show me that.
   ta üüniig nadad   Та үүнийг надад
   üzüülenüü?   үзүүлнэ үү?
It's too expensive.
   kheterkhii üntei bain   Хэтэрхий үнэтэй байна.
Have you got a cheaper one?
   tanaid arai khyamd   Танайд арай хямд
   bainuu?   байна уу?
Can you reduce the price?
   ta ün buulgakhuu?   Та үнэ буулгах уу?
I'll give you ... tughriks.
(see page 146 for numbers)
   bi tand ... tögrög ögökhüü?   Би танд ... төгрөг өгөх үү?

Souvenirs

The main hotels have 'dutyfree' shops where you can buy European and American beer, spirits and cigarettes, film, coffee and perfume, items of the colourful Mongolian national costume and other souvenirs. These shops have English-speaking staff and fixed prices in US dollars or sterling. You might find the same things cheaper if you have the time and patience to bargain with

SHOPPING

other local retailers. Traditional hats, leather boots and silk and leather jackets are popular, woollen carpets of various designs (mostly Genghis Khans these days, but a few Lenins still available), china figurines, attractive woodcarvings and water colours and excellent books of colour photos. And fur coats. Remember that the Mongols are close to nature and hunt wild animals to protect their livestock and provide themselves with warm clothing for the very severe winter.

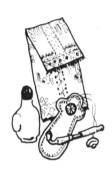

Water colours of country scenes are sold cheaper in the courtyards outside Gandan monastery *(Gandan khiid,* Гандан хийд) and the Bogd Khan's winter palace *(Bogd Khaany övliin ordon,* Богд хааны өвлийн ордон).

Mongolians who want to buy or sell things unavailable in the shops flock to the twice-weekly market in the northern suburbs. Once you have bought a ticket and fought your way inside the jampacked compound (hang on to your camera, wallet and watch), the choice is yours from the goods displayed on stalls or mats on the ground. A tap or bicycle chain, perhaps? Nails and screws? Old coins, banknotes or postage stamps? Bargain like fury, and don't flash your cash! Photography is discouraged.

Please show me some ...	*ta ... nadad üzüülenüü?*	Та ... надад үзүүлнэ үү?
books	*nom*	ном
carpets	*khivs*	хивс

SHOPPING

carvings	*siilber*	сийлбэр
earrings	*eemeg*	ээмэг
embroidery	*khatgamal*	хатгамал
fabrics	*daavuu*	даавуу
furniture	*tavilag*	тавилга
jewellery	*alt möngön edlel*	алт мөнгөн эдлэл
maps	*gazryn zurag*	газрын зураг
musical instruments	*khögjmiin zemseg*	хөгжмийн зэмсэг
paintings	*uran zurag*	уран зураг
souvenirs	*beleg dursgal*	бэлэг дурсгал
vodka	*arikh*	архи

Clothing

blouse	*emegtein tsamts*	эмэгтэйн цамц
bra	*khökhövch*	хөхөвч
clothing	*khuvtsas*	хувцас
coat	*pailto*	пальто
dress	*platye*	платье
gloves	*beelii*	бээлий
hat	*malgai*	малгай
jacket	*pidjak*	пиджак
jeans	*djins*	жинс
jumper	*nooson tsamts*	ноосон цамц
pyjamas	*untlagyn khuvtsas*	унтлагын хувцас
raincoat	*boroony tsuv*	борооны цув
sandals	*sandaal/ongorkhoi gutal*	сандаал/онгорхой гутал
scarf	*khüzüünii oroolt*	хүзүүний ороолт
shirt	*eregtein tsamts*	эрэгтэйн цамц
shoes	*gutal*	гутал
shorts	*bogin ömd*	богино өмд

skirt	*banzal*	банзал
socks/stockings	*oims*	ойм
suit	*kostyum*	костюм
swimsuit	*usny khuvtsas*	усны хувцас
trousers	*ömd*	өмд
underwear	*dotuur khuvtsas*	дотуур хувцас

Do you have any more of
these?
  tand en öör bainuu? Танд энэ өөр байна уу?
Can I try it on?
  bi ömsch üzej bolokhuu? Би өмсч үзэж болох уу?
Where is the mirror?
  toil khaa bain ve? Толь хаа байна вэ?
Where is the fitting room?
  ömsdög öröö khaa bain ve? Өмсдөг өрөө хаа байна вэ?
It fits well.
  saikhan taarch bain Сайхан таарч байна.
It doesn't fit.
  khemjee taarakhgüi bain Хэмжээ таарахгүй байна.

This is too ...	*en yum ... bain*	Энэ юм ... байна.
big	*tomdoj*	томдож
small	*bagadaj*	багадаж
long	*urtdaj*	уртдаж
short	*boginodoj*	богинодож
loose	*elbegdej*	элбэгдэж
tight	*baruudaj*	баруудаж

I would like to have these
clothes altered.
  bi en huvtssyg khasuulmaar Би энэ хувцсыг хасуулмаар
  bain байна.

Materials

cotton	*khövön daavuu*	хөвөн даавуу
handmade	*gar khiitsiin*	гар хийцийн
leather	*savikh*	савхи
linen	*yorog daavuu*	ёрог даавуу
satin	*atlaas daavuu*	атлаас даавуу
silk	*torog*	торго
wool	*nooson daavuu*	ноосон даавуу

Colours

black	*khar*	хар
blue	*khökh*	хөх
brown	*khüren*	хүрэн
dark blue	*khar khökh*	хар хөх
golden	*altan shar*	алтан шар
green	*nogoon*	ногоон
grey	*saaral/bor*	саарал/бор
light blue	*tsenkher*	цэнхэр
orange	*ulbar shar*	улбар шар
pink	*yagaan*	ягаан
red	*ulaan*	улаан
white	*tsagaan*	цагаан
yellow	*shar*	шар

Note that in Mongolian things are 'with ... colour' *(... öngtei)*.

Have you got another colour?
    öör öngtei bainuu?   Өөр өнгөтэй байна уу?

Stationery & Books

book	*nom*	ном
dictionary	*toil bichig*	толь бичиг

SHOPPING

drawing paper	*zurgiin tsaas*	зургийн цаас
exercise book	*devter*	дэвтэр
envelope	*dugtui*	дугтүй
eraser	*balluur*	баллуур
magazine	*setgüül*	сэтгүүл
map	*gazryn zurag*	газрын зураг
newspaper	*sonin*	сонин
newspaper in English	*angil khel deer gardag sonin*	англи хэл дээр гардаг сонин

notebook	*övriin devter*	өврийн дэвтэр
pen (ballpoint)	*toson bal*	тосон бал
pencil	*kharandaa*	харандаа
scissors	*khaich*	хайч
writing paper	*bichgiin tsaas*	бичгийн цаас

Photography

Since the delivery of a couple of processing machines you can
get your negative colour film developed and printed in Ulan Bator
if you want to, but you should take slide film home for
processing.

I'd like to have this film
developed.
    en khailsyg ugaalgi   Энэ хальсыг угаалгая.
How much do you charge?
    ta khedeer ugaakh ve?   Та хэдээр угаах вэ?
When will it be ready?
    khediid belen bolokh ve? Хэдийд бэлэн болох вэ?

B&W film	*khar tsagaan khails*	хар цагаан хальс
camera	*zurag avuur*	зураг авуур
colour film	*öngöt khails*	өнгөт хальс
colour slide film	*öngöt diapozitiv*	өнгөт диапозитив
film	*khails*	хальс
filter	*filtr*	фильтр
flash	*gyalbuur*	гялбуур
lens	*durang*	дуран
lens cap	*durangiin tag*	дурангийн таг
light meter	*gerel khemjüür*	гэрэл хэмжүүр

Smoking

a carton/box	*neg khairtsag*	нэг хайрцаг
cigarettes	*yanjuur*	янжуур
lighter	*asaaguur*	асаагуур
matches	*chüdenz*	чүдэнз
pipe	*gaans*	гаанс

A packet of cigarettes, please.
neg khairtsag yanjuur ögnüü?

Нэг хайрцаг янжуур өгнө үү?

Do you have a light?
ta galtai yuu?

Та галтай юу?

Weights & Measures

How much does this weigh?
en yamar jintei yum be?

Энэ ямар жинтэй юм бэ?

gram	*gram*	грамм
kilogram	*kilo*	кило
millimetre	*millimetr*	миллиметр
centimetre	*santimetr*	сантиметр
metre	*metr*	метр
kilometre	*kilometr*	километр
litre	*litr*	литр

square (kilo-) metre	*am (kilo-) metr*	ам (кило-) метр
cubic (centi-) metre	*shoo (santi-) metr*	шоо (санти-) метр

Sizes & Quantities

small	*jijig*	жижиг
smaller	*arai jijig*	арай жижиг
smallest	*khamgiin jijig*	хамгийн жижиг
big	*tom*	том
bigger	*arai tom*	арай том
biggest	*khamgiin tom*	хамгийн том
heavy	*khünd*	хүнд
light	*khöngöng*	хөнгөн
great	*ikh*	их

SHOPPING

little	*bag*	бага
more than that	*enees ikh*	энээс их
less than that	*enees bag*	энээс бага
many	*olon*	олон
too many	*dendüü olon*	дэндүү олон
long	*urt*	урт
short	*bogin*	богино
tall	*öndör*	өндөр
enough	*zügeer*	зүгээр
a little bit	*jaakhan*	жаахан

Some Useful Phrases

I don't like it.
  bi üünd durgüi bain Би үүнд дургүй байна.

Have you something of better quality?
  arai chanartai yum bainuu? Арай чанартай юм байна уу?

Please show me.
  nadad üzüülenüü? Надад үзүүлнэ үү?

I'll take (buy) it.
  üüniig avi! Үүнийг авъя!

There is none.
  baikhgüi Байхгүй.

Which one?
  aliin? Алий нь?

Can you write down the price?
  ta üniig bichij ögnüü? Та үнийг бичиж өгнө үү?

Can I pay by (credit) card?
  bi kartaar tölj bolokhuu? Би картаар төлж болох уу?

SHOPPING

Please pay cash.
ta belen möngöör tölönüü?   Та бэлэн мөнгөөр төлнө үү?

Please wrap it for me.
ta booj ögnüü?   Та боож өгнө үү?

Some Useful Words

backpack	*üürgevch*	үүргэвч
cheap	*khyamd*	хямд
handbag	*gar tsünkh*	гар цүнх
battery	*zai*	зай
bottle	*lonkh*	лонх
box	*khairtsag*	хайрцаг
button	*tovch*	товч
candle	*laa*	лаа
to discount	*khyamdruulakh*	хямдруулах
gold	*alt*	алт
mirror	*toil*	толь
receipt	*tasalbar*	тасалбар
to repair	*zasakh*	засах
silver	*möng*	мөнгө

SHOPPING

Health

Medical assistance can be obtained quite quickly and easily through emergency services in the capital and other principal towns, and some hotels have a doctor on hand. In the countryside help can be several hours away. Mongolian doctors have been trained in Western medicine. Tibetan traditional medicine is making something of a comeback but there are few practitioners. The chances of finding an English-speaking doctor outside Ulan Bator are remote, although some medical personnel understand German or Russian. You may have to pay for medical attention.

Shortages of drugs and instruments and delapidated facilities have lowered standards of medical care. Avoid blood transfusion except in an emergency. In the event of a serious accident or illness you would be wise to arrange evacuation, so you should consider beforehand whether special insurance cover may be needed for a long stay or travel to remote areas. No special vaccinations have been required on entry for visitors from Europe, North America, Australia or Japan.

Mongolia is generally speaking a healthy country, but some visitors prefer to innoculate themselves against hepatitis and tetanus. Seek up-to-date advice from your own physician. Minor outbreaks of plague in country areas in recent years have been associated with eating marmot meat. You can drink from the mains water supply in Ulan Bator, but you should avoid drinking from streams and other sources of unboiled water. The Mongolian concept of hygiene falls short of European ideals. Home-made dairy products may cause stomach upsets.

I'm not feeling well.
minii bii muu bain Миний бие муу байна.

My friend is sick.
minii nökhriin bii muu bain Миний нөхрийн бие муу байна.

Send for a doctor.
emchid khün yavuuli Эмчид хүн явуулъя.

We need an English-speaking doctor.
bidend angliar yardag emch kheregtei bain Бидэнд англиар ярьдаг эмч хэрэгтэй байна.

I would like to be examined by a female doctor.
bi emegtei emcheer üzüülmeer bain Би эмэгтэй эмчээр үзүүлмээр байна.

Where is ...? *... khaan bain ve?* ... хаана байна вэ?
a doctor *emch* Эмч
the hospital *emneleg* Эмнэлэг
the chemist *emiin sang* Эмийн сан

Symptoms

I feel dizzy.
minii tolgoi ergeed bain Миний толгой эргээд байна.

I feel very weak.
bi ikh tamirdaad bain Би их тамирдаад байна.

My whole body aches.
minii khamag bii
sharkhiraad bain

Миний хамаг бие
шархираад байна.

I have a temperature.
bi khaluuraad bain

Би халуураад байна.

I have been having heart
pains.
minii zürkheer üi üi
khatgaj övdÖÖd bain

Миний зүрхээр үе үе
хатгаж өвдөөд байна.

I feel sick.
minii bÖÖljis tsutgaad
bain

Миний бөөлжис цутгаад
байна.

I can't sleep.
bi untaj chadakhgüi bain

Би унтаж чадахгүй байна.

It hurts here.
end Övdöj bain

Энд өвдөж байна.

I am bleeding.
tsus aldsan

Цус алдсан.

Complaints

I've been bitten by a snake
(stung/bitten by an insect).
bi mogoid (neg shaivjind)
khatguulchikhlaa

Би могойд (нэг шавьжинд)
хатгуулчихлаа.

It's ...

broken	*khugarsan*	Хугарсан.
burned	*tülegdsen*	Түлэгдсэн.
cut	*ogtolson*	Огтолсон.
dislocated	*multarsan*	Мултарсан.
frostbitten	*khÖldÖÖsön*	Хөлдөөсөн.

HEALTH

| sprained | *bulgarsan* | Булгарсан. |
| swollen | *khavdsan* | Хавдсан. |

I have ...
concussion	*minii tarikh khödölsön*	Миний тархи хөдөлсөн.
constipation	*minii ötgön khataad bain*	Миний өтгөн хатаад байна.
diarrhoea	*bi suulgaad bain*	Би суулгаад байна.

I have ...   *bi ... tussan*   Би ... туссан.
asthma	*bügshikh menger*	бүгших мэнгэр
food poisoning	*khoolny khordlog*	хоолны хордлого
haemorrhoids	*shambaram*	шамбарам
meningitis	*meningit*	менингит
pneumonia	*uushigny khatgalgaa*	уушигны хатгалгаа
marmot plague	*tarvagan takhal*	тарваган тахал
rabies	*galzuu*	галзуу
tetanus	*tatran*	татран
tuberculosis	*süryii*	сүрьеэ
typhoid	*gedesnii khijig*	гэдэсний хижиг

I am suffering from ...   *bi ... övchind shanalj bain*   Би ... өвчинд шаналж байна.
hepatitis	*elegnii*	элэгний
rheumatism	*üi möchnii*	үе мөчний
venereal disease	*öngönii*	өнгөний

HEALTH

Women's Health

I'm on the pill.
  bi jiremslelkhees   Би жирэмслэлхээс
  khamgaalakh ürel   хамгаалах үрэл хэрэглэдэг.
  kheregledeg
I'm pregnant.
  bi jiremsen   Би жирэмсэн.
I haven't had my period for ...
months.
  minii saryn temdeg ... sar   Миний сарын тэмдэг ... сар
  ireegüi   ирээгүй.
I've had a miscarriage.
  ür zulbasan   Үр зулбасан.

gynaecologist	*emegteichüüdiin emch*	эмэгтэйчүүдийн эмч
maternity hospital	*amarjikh gazar*	амаржих газар
menstruation	*saryn temdeg*	сарын тэмдэг
midwife	*ekh barigch*	эх баригч
pregnant	*jiremsen*	жирэмсэн
stillbirth	*aimgüi khuüükhed törüülekh*	амьгүй хүүхэд төрүүлэх

Allergies

I'm allergic to ...   *minii bied ...*   Миний биед ...
                       harshdag   харшдаг.

    antibiotics   *antibiotik*   антибиотик
    aspirin   *aspirin*   аспирин
    penicillin   *penitsilin*   пеницилин

Parts of the Body

My ... hurts.	*minii ... övdöj bain*	Миний ... өвдөж байна.
abdomen	*khevlii*	хэвлий
ankle	*shagai*	шагай
appendix	*mukhar olgoi*	мухар олгой
bladder	*davsag*	давсаг
blood	*tsus*	цус

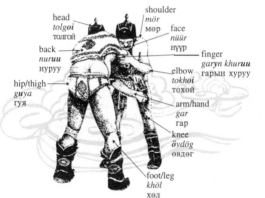

head
tolgoi
толгой

back
nuruu
нуруу

hip/thigh
guya
гуя

shoulder
mör
мөр

face
nüür
нүүр

finger
garyn khuruu
гарын хуруу

elbow
tokhoi
тохой

arm/hand
gar
гар

knee
övdög
өвдөг

foot/leg
khöl
хөл

bone	*yas*	яс
bowels	*gedes dotor*	гэдэс дотор
brain	*uurag tarikh*	уураг тархи
breast	*khökh*	хөх
chest	*tseej*	цээж
ear	*chikh*	чих
eye	*nüd*	нүд
hand/arm	*gar*	гар

heart	*zürkh*	зүрх
kidney	*böör*	бөөр
leg/foot	*khöl*	хөл
liver	*eleg*	элэг
lung	*uushig*	уушиг
mouth	*am*	ам
muscle	*bulching*	булчин
neck	*khüzüü*	хүзүү
nose	*khamar*	хамар
rib	*khavirag*	хавирга
skin	*aris*	арьс
spine	*nuruu*	нуруу
stomach	*gedes*	гэдэс
tooth	*shüd*	шүд
thigh/hip	*guya*	гуя
throat	*khooloi*	хоолой
thumb	*garyn erkhii khuruu*	гарын эрхий хуруу
toe	*khöliin khuruu*	хөлийн хуруу
toe (big)	*khöliin erkhii khuruu*	хөлийн эрхий хуруу
tongue	*khel*	хэл
wrist	*bugui*	бугуй

At the Chemist

Chemists in Mongolian towns usually have a small range of mostly unfamiliar drugs, medicines and surgical equipment from Russia and China. The counter display may also include imported shampoos, sprays, condoms, stockings, shaving gear and combs, but probably not tampons, film, toilet paper or tissues. Bring with you a full supply of any prescribed drugs, plus other pills or

HEALTH

ointments you may need, as well as spare spectacles, contact lenses, false teeth or hearing-aid batteries.

chemist/pharmacy	*emiin sang*	эмийн сан
Have you got ...?	*tanaid ... bainuu?*	Танайд ... байна уу?
Please give me ...	*nadad ... ögnüü?*	Надад ... өгнө үү?
antiseptic	*örövsliin em*	өрөвслийн эм
aspirin	*aspirin*	аспирин
baby's bottle	*ugj*	угж
comb	*sam*	сам
condom	*belgevch*	бэлгэвч
contraceptive	*jiremslekhees khamgaalakh züil*	жирэмслэхээс хамгаалах зүйл
cotton wool	*khövön*	хөвөн
cough mixture	*khaniadny em*	ханиадны эм
deodorant	*dezodront*	дэзодронт
diaper/nappy	*chivkh*	чивх
disinfectant	*ariutgalyn bodis*	ариутгалын бодис
eyedrops	*nüdnii dusaal*	нүдний дусаал
hairbrush	*üsnii soiz*	үсний сойз
insect repellant	*shavij ustgakh bodis*	шавьж устгах бодис
laxative	*tuulag*	туулга
ointment	*toson em*	тосон эм
painkiller	*övchin namdaakh em*	өвчин намдаах эм
prescription	*emiin jor*	эмийн жор
razor	*khusuur*	хусуур
razor blade	*sakhlyn khutag*	сахлын хутга
sanitary towel	*emegteichüüdiin khereglel*	эмэгтэйчүүдийн хэрэглэл
sedative	*taivshruulakh em*	тайвшруулах эм

shampoo	*shampuin*	шампунь
shaving soap	*sakhlyn savang*	сахлын саван
sleeping pill/ draught	*noiryn em*	нойрын эм
sticking plaster	*lent/naaltaas*	лент/наалтаас
suntan cream	*narny tos*	нарны тос
tablet	*ürel*	үрэл
tampon	*khövön böglöös*	хөвөн бөглөөс
teat	*ugjiin khökh*	угжийн хөх
thermometer	*khaluuny shil*	халууны шил
tissues	*tsaasan alchuur*	цаасан алчуур
toilet paper	*jorlongiin tsaas*	жорлонгийн цаас
toothbrush	*shüdnii soiz*	шүдний сойз
toothpaste	*shüdnii oo*	шүдний оо
vaseline	*vazelin*	вазелин
vitamin	*vitamin*	витамин

At the Dentist

When does the dentist see patients?

shüdnii emch khediid üzdeg yum be?   Шүдний эмч хэдийд үздэг юм бэ?

I have a toothache.

minii shüd övdöj bain   Миний шүд өвдөж байна.

My ... hurts.	*minii ... övdöj bain*	Миний ... өвдөж байна.
upper tooth	*deed shüd*	дээд шүд
lower tooth	*dood shüd*	доод шүд
front tooth (incisor)	*üüden shüd*	үүдэн шүд
back tooth (molar)	*araa*	араа

The filling has fallen out.
   böglöösen unachikhlaa
I don't want it extracted.
   *minii en shüdiig bitgii
avaach*
Please give me a filling.
   nadad böglöj ögnüü?
Please give me an anaesthetic.
   *nadad medee alduulakh
taria khiij ögnüü?*

Бөглөөс нь уначихлаа.

Миний энэ шүдийг битгий
аваач.

Надад бөглөж өгнө үү?

Надад мэдээ алдуулах
тариа хийж өгнө үү?

Other Medical Terms

abortion	*ür khöndüülekh*	үр хөндүүлэх
acid	*khüchil*	хүчил
acupuncture	*züü tavikh*	зүү тавих
acute	*khurts*	хурц
AIDS	*darkhlal khomsdolyn kham shinj övchin*	дархлал хомсдолын хам шинж (ДХХШ) өвчин
alkali	*shült*	шүлт
allergy	*harshil*	харшил
ambulance	*türgen tuslamjiin mashin*	түргэн тусламжийн машин
amputation	*erkhten tairakh*	эрхтэн тайрах
anaesthetic (general)	*noirsuulakh*	нойрсуулах
anaesthetic (local)	*khesgiin medee alduulakh*	хэсгийн мэдээ алдуулах
antibiotic	*antibiotik*	антибиотик
antiseptic	*örövsliin em*	өрөвслийн эм
artery	*taraakh sudas*	тараах судас

HEALTH

artificial respiration	*khiimel aimsgal*	хиймэл амьсгал
bandage	*boolt*	боолт
blister	*tsevrüü*	цэврүү
blood group	*tsusny büleg*	цусны бүлэг
blood pressure	*tsusny daralt*	цусны даралт
blood test	*tsusny shinjilgee*	цусны шинжилгээ
blood transfusion	*tsus khiikh*	цус хийх
chronic	*arkhag*	архаг
cramp (have)	*bulchin agshikh*	булчин агших
crutches	*almuur*	алмуур
diabetes	*chikhriin*	чихрийн
diagnosis	*onosh*	онош
faeces	*baas*	баас
heart attack	*zürkhnii bagtraa*	зүрхний багтраа

hospital	*emneleg*	эмнэлэг
infection	*khaldvar*	халдвар
injection	*tarilag*	тарилга
lose consciousness	*ukhaan aldakh*	ухаан алдах
medicine	*em*	эм
needle (hypo)	*tariany züü*	тарианы зүү
nurse	*suvilagch*	сувилагч
ointment	*toson em*	тосон эм
operation	*khagalgaa*	хагалгаа
oxygen	*khüchiltörögch*	хүчилтөрөгч
patient	*övchtön*	өвчтөн
plaster cast	*göltgönön boolt*	гөлтгөнөн боолт
poison	*khor*	хор
pulse	*sudasny tsokhilt*	судасны цохилт
pus	*idee beer*	идээ бээр
rash	*bijrüü*	бижрүү
serious	*khünd*	хүнд
stitch	*oyodlyn utas*	оёдлын утас
stretcher	*damnuurag*	дамнуурга
surgery	*mes zasal*	мэс засал
urine	*shees*	шээс
vaccine	*vaktsin*	вакцин
vein	*khuraakh sudas*	хураах судас
wound	*sharkh*	шарх

Time, Dates & Holidays

Telling the Time

Telling the time is quite easy once you've learnt the numbers. You can just say 3.20 or half four (lit: four half) as you would in English (see examples below). If you say *tsag* for the hours and *minut* for the minutes past the hour, remember to use the *-n* forms of the numbers (see Numbers chapter). It is usual to add at the end the verb form used for time expressions – *bolj bain*. The 24-hour clock is used at airports and railway stations.

What time is it?
kheden tsag bolj bain?   Хэдэн цаг болж байна?

9 am	*yösön tsag bolj bain*	Есөн цаг болж байна.
12(noon)	*üdiin arvan khoyor tsag bolj bain*	Үдийн арван хоёр цаг болж байна.
1.10	*neg tsag arvan minut bolj bain*	Нэг цаг арван минут болж байна.
2.15	*khoyor tsag arvan tavan minut bolj bain*	Хоёр цаг арван таван минут болж байна.
3.20	*gurav khori bolj bain*	Гурав хорь болж байна.
4.30	*döröv khagas bolj bain*	Дөрөв хагас болж байна.

136

4.55	*tavan tsagt tavan minut dutuu bain*	Таван цагт таван минут дутуу байна.
5.40	*tavan tsag döchin minut bolj bain*	Таван цаг дөчин минут болж байна.
6.45	*zurgaan tsag döchin tavan minut bolj bain*	Зургаан цаг дөчин таван минут болж байна.

If you ask when (at what time) something is happening, the words *tsag*, *khagas*, etc and the numbers need to be changed a bit:

When?	*kheded?*	Хэдэд?
At ten.	*aravd*	Арвад.
At what time?	*kheden tsagt?*	Хэдэн цагт?
At ten o'clock.	*arvan tsagt*	Арван цагт.

At half past five.
  tav khagast   Тав хагаст.
At 5.30.
  tav guchid   Тав гучид.
At five hours 30 minutes.
(5.30)
  tavan tsag guchin minutad   Таван цаг гучин минутад.

hour	*tsag*	цаг
minute	*minut*	минут
second	*sekund*	секунд
half-hour	*khagas tsag*	хагас цаг

am
üdees ömön
үдээс өмнө

morning
öglöö
өглөө

pm
üdees khoish
үдээс хойш

evening
oroi
орой

afternoon
ödör
өдөр

The animal names of the lunar years (see Lunar Calendar, page 139) are also used in the same order for the traditional division of the day into 12 two-hour 'hours', beginning with the 'tiger hour' from 3 to 5 am. This may be based on the movement of sunlight entering the yurt or *ger* through the skylight or *toon* (тооно) and passing during the day across various points of the compass named according to the animal cycle.

Days

Monday	*davaa*	даваа
Tuesday	*myagmar*	мягмар
Wednesday	*lkhavag*	лхагва
Thursday	*pürev*	пүрэв
Friday	*baasang*	баасан
Saturday	*byamb*	бямба
Sunday	*nyam*	ням

The word *garig* (гариг or гараг) meaning 'planet' is often added: *davaa garig* (даваа гариг) is Monday. The days can also simply be numbered from first to seventh (from Monday) using the short form of the ordinal numbers (see Numbers). The answer will be in this form if you ask:

What day is it today?
önöödör kheddekh ödör ve? Өнөөдөр хэддэх өдөр вэ?
Today is Friday.
önöödör tavdakh ödör Өнөөдөр тавдахь өдөр.
(today fifth day)

Sunday, which is a day off work for most urban Mongols, is also called 'the good day' or *sain ödör* (сайн өдөр). Saturday, when they usually work a half-day, is therefore called 'the half good day' or *khagas sain ödör* (хагас сайн өдөр). The other days of the week are working days or *ajlyn ödör* (ажлын өдөр). Holidays are *amraltyn ödör* (амралтын өдөр).

Another set of planetary names for days of the week is less common but also in use (one is Tibetan, the other Sanskrit): *sumyaa* (сумъяа), *angarag* (ангараг), *bud* (буд), *barkhasbadi* (бархасбадь), *sugar* (сугар), *sanchir* (санчир) and *adyaa* (адьяа). The original meanings are the same for both sets: Moon, Mars, Mercury, Jupiter, Venus, Saturn and Sun. Often Mongolians are named after the day of the week on which they were born.

Lunar Calendar

The calendar in general use in Mongolia nowadays is the modern solar (Gregorian) calendar, and anniversaries and other official dates are set by it. However, religious festivals and in particular the Mongolian Buddhist new year holiday 'White Moon' (*tsagaan sar*, цагаан сар) are celebrated according to the lunar calendar. The Mongolian new year falls in January or February depending on the phases of the moon and is mostly celebrated at the same

TIME, DATES & HOLIDAYS

time as the Chinese new year, unless the leap year has been calculated differently.

The Mongolian lunar calendar, like similar Chinese and Tibetan calendars, is based on cycles of 12 years named after animals – tiger, hare, dragon, snake, horse, sheep, monkey, chicken, dog, pig, mouse and ox. The years are alternately male and female, so that for example the tiger year is male and the hare female; the sheep, chicken, pig and ox years are sometimes called ewe, hen, sow or cow years in English.

Each animal in turn is combined with an element (wood, fire, earth, iron and water) and a colour (blue, red, yellow, white and black) which change every two years. For example, the lunar year 1994 to 1995 is the 'blue wooden dog' year, 95-96 the 'blue wooden sow' year, and 96-97 the 'fiery red mouse' year. The combinations of 12 animals and five elements (colours) produce 60 uniquely named years called a *jaran,* жаран (60) or 'Mongolian (Buddhist) century'. The current *jaran* is the 17th.

Months

January	*negdügeer sar*	нэгдүгээр сар
February	*khoyordugaar sar*	хоёрдугаар сар
March	*guravdugaar sar*	гуравдугаар сар
April	*dörövdügeer sar*	дөрөвдүгээр сар
May	*tavdugaar sar*	тавдугаар сар
June	*zurgadugaar sar*	зургадугаар сар
July	*doldugaar sar*	долдугаар сар
August	*naimdugaar sar*	наймдугаар сар
September	*yösdügeer sar*	есдүгээр сар
October	*aravdugaar sar*	аравдугаар сар
November	*arvannegdügeer sar*	арваннэгдүгээр сар
December	*arvankhoyordugaar sar*	арванхоёрдугаар сар

The months or *sar* (сар), 'moons' of the modern calendar are numbered from first to 12th, using ordinal numbers. Months numbered in the *-n* form of the cardinal numbers (see the Numbers chapter), eg 'first moon' (*neg sar*, нэг сар) or 'third moon' (*gurvan sar*, гурван сар) refer to the months of the lunar calendar. The animal names of the lunar years (see above) are also sometimes given in the same order to lunar months.

Dates

Dates in the modern style start with the year, followed by the month and then the day: 11th July 1996 in Mongolian is *myang yösön zuun yören zurgaan ony doldugaar saryn arvan negen* (мянга есөн зуун ерэн зургаан оны долдугаар сарын арван нэгэн), that is 'thousand nine hundred ninetyfour year's seventh month's eleven'. Note that in dates the word for 'year' is *on* (он), but 'this year' is *en jil* (энэ жил) and 'next year' *irekh jil* (ирэх жил).

What date is it today?
 önöödör kheden be?   Өнөөдөр хэдэн бэ?
Today is 13th January.
 önöödör negdügeer saryn   Өнөөдөр нэгдүгээр сарын
 arvan gurvan   арван гурван.
Tomorrow is 26th November.
 margaash arvannegdügeer   Маргааш арваннэгдүгээр
 saryn khorin zurgaan   сарын хорин зургаан.

Present

today/this afternoon	*önöödör*	өнөөдөр
this morning	*önöö öglöö*	өнөө өглөө
this evening	*önöö üdesh*	өнөө үдэш

tonight	*önöö oroi*	өнөө орой
this week	*en doloo khonog*	энэ долоо хоног
this month	*en sar*	энэ сар
this year	*en jil*	энэ жил
immediately	*odookhon*	одоохон
now	*odoo*	одоо

Past

yesterday	*öchigdör*	өчигдөр
day before yesterday	*urjigdar*	уржигдар
yesterday morning	*öchigdör öglöö*	өчигдөр өглөө
yesterday afternoon	*öchigdör ödör*	өчигдөр өдөр
yesterday evening	*öchigdör üdesh*	өчигдөр үдэш
last night	*urd shön*	урд шөнө
last week	*öngörsön doloo khonog*	өнгөрсөн долоо хоног
last month	*öngörsön sar*	өнгөрсөн сар
last year	*öngörsön jil*	өнгөрсөн жил

Future

tomorrow	*margaash*	маргааш
day after tomorrow	*nögöödör*	нөгөөдөр
tomorrow morning	*margaash öglöö*	маргааш өглөө
tomorrow afternoon	*margaash ödör*	маргааш өдөр
tomorrow evening	*margaash oroi*	маргааш орой
tomorrow night	*margaash shön*	маргааш шөнө
next week	*daraa doloo khonog*	дараа долоо хоног
next month	*daraa sar*	дараа сар
next year	*daraa jil*	дараа жил

Some Useful Words

afterwards	*daraa*	дараа
always	*dandaa*	дандаа
beforehand	*uirdaar*	урьдаар
century	*zuun*	зуун
day	*ödör*	өдөр
a day and a night (24 hours)	*khonog*	хоног
early	*ert*	эрт
every day	*ödör bür*	өдөр бүр
midnight	*shön dund*	шөн дунд
month	*sar*	сар
night	*shön*	шөнө
noon	*üd*	үд
permanently	*bainga*	байнга
recently	*sayakhan*	саяхан
sunrise	*nar mandakh*	нар мандах
sunset	*nar jargakh*	нар жаргах
week	*doloo khonog*	долоо хоног
year	*jil*	жил

Seasons

spring	*khavar*	хавар
summer	*zun*	зун
autumn	*namar*	намар
winter	*övöl*	өвөл

Festivals & Holidays

Mongolia's festivals are based on traditions going back to the times of Genghis Khan, and religious practices developed from Lamaism (Tibetan Buddhism) since the 16th century. The rebirth of religious freedom in the 1990s has encouraged the growth of Lamaism and the restoration of monasteries and temples, and religious festivals are held regularly according to the Buddhist calendar, although most people consider them a matter of tradition rather than faith. Genghis Khan is being turned into a tourist attraction and his birth anniversary is now celebrated in May each year.

tsagaan sar   цагаан сар
The new year festival according to the lunar calendar (see above), held in January or February. This is a big family celebration lasting three days with various ceremonies, visits to relatives, exchanges of gifts and lots of eating and especially drinking. Devout Lamaists attend their local temple.

naadam   наадам
The national festival of 'three manly sports' – wrestling, archery and horseracing – beginning on 11th July. Under the old communist regime *naadam* used to be preceded by military parades and workers' demonstrations in central Ulan Bator's Sükhbaatar Square (Сухбаатарын талбай) to mark the anniversary of the establishment in 1921 of Mongolia's revolutionary government. Nowadays the Mongolian President opens the three-day festival at the city stadium with a colourful ceremony combining national and quasi-religious elements. The serious drinking is done at the horseherds' camp out towards Ulan Bator's Buyant-Ukhaa (Буянт-ухаа) airport.

shin jil   шинэ жил
Mongolians also have a one-day new year's holiday on 1st January. The aim is to get three days' drinking done in one day.

Three anniversaries are celebrated but are not public holidays: 13th January, marking the adoption of the country's new Constitution in 1992; 26th November, now called Republic Day, marking the adoption of the country's first Constitution in 1924; and 8th March, International Women's Day, a communist-inspired occasion when the male half of the population gives flowers to the female half to make up for their drunkenness over the rest of the year.

Numbers & Amounts

The system of numbers in Mongolian is logical and regular within its own rules. Generally except for two (and compound numbers including two), Mongolian numbers add a final -*n* when they are followed by another number or an object. For example, while 10 is *arav* (арав), 11 is *arvan neg* (арван нэг) and 18 is *arvan naim* (арван найм); 30 is *guch* (гуч) but 32 is *guchin khoyor* (гучин хоёр); 300 is *gurvan zuu* (гурван зуу), etc. Note the special units for 10,000 (*tümen*, түмэн), 100,000 (*buman*, буман) and 100 million (*dünchüür*, дүнчүүр).

Cardinal Numbers

0	*teg*	тэг
1	*neg*	нэг
2	*khoyor*	хоёр
3	*gurav*	гурав
4	*döröv*	дөрөв
5	*tav*	тав
6	*zurgaa*	зургаа
7	*doloo*	долоо
8	*naim*	найм
9	*yös*	ес

10	*a*rav	арав
11	*a*rvan neg	арван нэг
12	*a*rvan kho*y*or	арван хоёр
13	*a*rvan *g*urav	арван гурав
14	*a*rvan dö*r*öv	арван дөрөв
15	*a*rvan tav	арван тав
16	*a*rvan zurgaa	арван зургаа
17	*a*rvan doloo	арван долоо
18	*a*rvan naim	арван найм
19	*a*rvan yös	арван ес
20	khori	хорь
21	khorin neg	хорин нэг
22	khorin kho*y*or	хорин хоёр
30	guch	гуч
31	*gu*chin neg	гучин нэг
40	döch	дөч
41	*d*öchin neg	дөчин нэг
50	taiv	тавь
51	ta*v*in neg	тавин нэг
60	jar	жар
61	*j*aran neg	жаран нэг
70	dal	дал
71	dalan neg	далан нэг
80	nai	ная
81	nain neg	наян нэг
90	yör	ер
91	yören neg	ерэн нэг
100	zuu	зуу
101	neg zuun neg	нэг зуун нэг
110	neg zuun arav	нэг зуун арав
111	neg zuun *a*rvan neg	нэг зуун арван нэг
200	kho*y*or zuu	хоёр зуу

201	*khoyor zuun neg*	хоёр зуун нэг
300	*gurvan zuu*	гурван зуу
400	*dörvön zuu*	дөрвөн зуу
500	*tavan zuu*	таван зуу
600	*zurgaan zuu*	зургаан зуу
700	*doloon zuu*	долоон зуу
800	*naiman zuu*	найман зуу
900	*yösön zuu*	есөн зуу
1000	*myang*	мянга
1,995	*neg myang yösön*	нэг мянга есөн
	zuun yören tav	зуун ерэн тав
2000	*khoyor myang*	хоёр мянга
3000	*gurvan myang*	гурван мянга
10,000	*tümen/arvan myang*	түмэн/арван мянга
100,000	*buman/zuun myang*	буман/зуун мянга
one million	*sai*	сая
two million	*khoyor sai*	хоёр сая
100 million	*dünchüür/zuun sai*	дүнчүүр/зуун сая
one billion	*terbum*	тэрбум

Note that Mongolians do not use a comma but may use a space to separate thousands and millions (1 000 000 000).

Fractions

half	*khagas*	хагас
one-third	*gurvany neg*	гуравны нэг ('of three one')
a quarter	*dörvönii neg*	дөрөвний нэг ('of four one')
three-quarters	*dörvönii gurav*	дөрөвний гурав
		('of four three')

Decimals

In writing decimals Mongolians put a comma where English-speakers use a stop:

4,9
dörvön bükhel aravny yös   дөрвөн бүхэл аравны ес
                             ('four whole of ten nine')

0,12
teg bükhel zuuny arvan   тэг бухэл зууны арван хоёр
khoyor   ('zero whole of hundred twelve')

Ordinal Numbers

These are formed by adding *-dügeer* (-дүгээр) to front-vowel numbers and *-dugaar* (-дугаар) to back-vowel numbers. Note that 6th and 7th lose their long vowels:

1st	*negdügeer*	нэгдүгээр
2nd	*khoyordugaar*	хоёрдугаар
3rd	*guravdugaar*	гуравдугаар
4th	*dörövdügeer*	дөрөвдүгээр
5th	*tavdugaar*	тавдугаар
6th	*zurgadugaar*	зургадугаар
7th	*doldugaar*	долдугаар
8th	*naimdugaar*	наймдугаар
9th	*yösdügeer*	есдүгээр
10th	*aravdugaar*	аравдугаар
11th	*arvannegdügeer*	арваннэгдүгээр

There are common alternative short forms: 1st, *negdekh* (нэгдэх); 2nd, *khoyordakh* (хоёрдахь); 3rd, *guravdakh* (гуравдахь); 4th,

NUMBERS

dörövdekh (дөрөвдэх), etc which are also used for the days of the week (see the Time & Dates chapter, page 138). Yet another form of first is *ankhny* (анхны), meaning 'original' or 'initial' rather than first of a series.

Some Useful Words

once/on one occasion	*neg udaa*	нэг удаа
twice	*khoyor udaa*	хоёр удаа
double/twice as much	*khoyor dakhin ilüü*	хоёр дахин илүү
more	*ilüü*	илүү
less	*dutuu*	дутуу
about	*... orchim*	... орчим
How many?	*kheden?*	Хэдэн?
little	*bag*	бага
few	*tsöön*	цөөн
many	*olon*	олон
percent	*khuiv*	хувь
pair	*khos*	хос

Vocabulary

In the following list, some words have three dots (ellipses) before or after them. This is to indicate where the word they refer to should go.

A

abacus	*samping*	сампин
able (be; can)	*khiij chadakh*	хийж чадах
about (approximately)	*orchim*	орчим
above/on	*... deer*	... дээр
accept	*hüleen avakh*	хүлээн авах
ache	*övdökh*	өвдөх
actor	*jüjigchin*	жүжигчин
adaptor	*tokhiruulagch*	тохируулагч
accident (mishap)	*osol*	осол
accident (traffic)	*avaair*	аваарь
accommodation	*bair*	байр
address	*hayag*	хаяг
admission (entry)	*orokh bolomj*	орох боломж
aeroplane	*nisekh ongots*	нисэх онгоц
afraid (be)	*aikh*	айх
after	*... daraa*	... дараа
again	*dakhiad*	дахиад

151

against	... *esreg*	... эсрэг
age	*nas*	нас
agree	*zövshöörökh*	зөвшөөрөх
agriculture	*khödöö aj akhui*	хөдөө аж ахуй
air	*agaar*	агаар
air-conditioning	*agaarjuulalt*	агааржуулалт
airmail	*agaaryn shuudang*	агаарын шуудан
airport	*nisekh ongotsny buudal*	нисэх онгоцны буудал
alarm clock	*serüülegtey tsag*	сэрүүлэгтэй цаг
all	*bükh*	бүх
almost	*barag*	бараг
alone	*gantsaar*	ганцаар
already	*hediinee*	хэдийнээ
also	*bas*	бас
alter	*öörchlökh*	өөрчлөх
always	*golduu*	голдуу
am/is/are	*bain*	байна
ambassador	*elchin said*	элчин сайд
ancient	*ertnii*	эртний
and	*ba*	ба
angry	*uurtai*	уртай
animal	*aimtan*	амьтан
animal husbandry	*mal aj akhui*	мал аж ахуй
answer (v)	*khariulakh*	хариулах
antique	*ertnii ed khereglel*	эртний эд хэрэглэл
appointment	*uulzalt*	уулзалт
arable	*gazar tarialan*	газар тариалан
archaeology	*arkheologi*	археологи
archery	*kharvalag*	харвалга
architecture	*uran barilag*	уран барилга

are/is/am	*bain*	байна
argue	*margakh*	маргах
around	*... ergen toiron*	... эргэн тойрон
arrive	*hüreltsen irekh*	хүрэлцэн ирэх
arrow	*sum*	сум
art (fine)	*dürslekh urlag*	дүрслэх урлаг
artist	*zuraach*	зураач
arts & crafts	*gar urlal*	гар урлал
ashtray	*ünsnii sav*	үнсний сав
ask	*asuukh*	асуух
atheist	*burkhangüi*	бурхангүй
automatic	*avtomat*	автомат
autumn	*namar*	намар

B

baby	*nyalkh khüükhed*	нялх хүүхэд
baby food	*nyalkh khüükhdiin khool*	нялх хүүхдийн хоол
babysitter	*khüükhed asragch*	хүүхэд асрагч
back (rear)	*hoid*	хойд
backpack	*üürgevch*	үүргэвч
bad	*muu*	муу
bag	*uut*	уут
baggage	*achaa*	ачаа
balcony	*tagt*	тагт
ball	*bömbög*	бөмбөг
bank	*bank*	банк
banknote	*möngön temdegt*	мөнгөн тэмдэгт
bar (drinks)	*baar*	баар
barber's	*üschinii gazar*	үсчний газар
basin	*gadar*	гадар

bathing suit	*usny khuvtsas*	усны хувцас
bathroom	*ugaalgyn öröö*	угаалгын өрөө
battery	*zai*	зай
bazaar	*zakh*	зах
be (v)	*bain*	байна
beard	*sakhal*	сахал
beautiful	*saikhan*	сайхан
because	*... uchraas*	... учраас
bed	*or*	ор
bedbug	*byasaa*	бясаа
bedroom	*untlagyn öröö*	унтлагын өрөө
before	*... ömön*	... өмнө
beggar	*guilgaching*	гуйлгачин
begin	*ekhlekh*	эхлэх
behind	*... khoin*	... хойно
bell	*khonkh*	хонх
below	*... dor*	... дор
beside	*derged*	дэргэд
best	*khamgiin sain*	хамгийн сайн
better	*davuu*	давуу
bicycle	*unadag dugui*	унадаг дугуй
big	*tom*	том
bigger	*ilüü*	илүү
bill (check)	*tootsoo*	тооцоо
bill (note)	*möngön temdegt*	мөнгөн тэмдэгт
birthday	*törsön ödör*	төрсөн өдөр
bite	*zuukh*	зуух
bitter	*gashuun*	гашуун
black	*khar*	хар
blanket	*khönjil*	хөнжил
blind	*kharaagüi*	хараагүй
blouse	*(emegtein) tsamts*	(эмэгтэйн) цамц

blue (dark)	*khökh*	хөх
blue (light)	*tsenkher*	цэнхэр
boat	*(usny) ongots*	(усны) онгоц
body	*bii*	бие
boil (bring to)	*butsalgakh*	буцалгах
boiled water	*butsalgasan us*	буцалгасан ус
bomb	*bömbög*	бөмбөг
bone	*yas*	яс
book	*nom*	ном
bookshop	*nomyn delgüür*	номын дэлгүүр
boot	*gutal*	гутал
border	*khil*	хил
bored	*uitgartai*	уйтгартай
borrow (use)	*tür avch khereglekh*	түр авч хэрэглэх
borrow (bank loan)	*zeelekh*	зээлэх
boss (n)	*ezen*	эзэн
bottle	*shil/lonkh*	шил/лонх
bottle (baby's)	*ugj*	угж
bottle-opener	*böglöö ongoilguur*	бөглөө онгойлгуур
bow (archery)	*num*	ном
bowl	*ayag*	аяга
box	*khairtsag*	хайрцаг
boy	*khüü*	хүү
bracelet	*buguivch*	бугуйвч
bread	*talkh*	талх
breakfast	*öglöönii und*	өглөөний унд
breathe	*aimsgaalakh*	амьсгаалах
bribe	*kheel khakhuuil*	хээл хахууль
bridge	*güür*	гүүр
bridle	*khazaar*	хазаар
briefcase	*tsünkh*	цүнх
bright (clever)	*sergeleng*	сэргэлэн

VOCABULARY

bright (shiny)	*gyalalzsan*	гялалзсан
bring	*avchrakh*	авчрах
broken (bone)	*khugarsan*	хугарсан
broken (out of order)	*ajillakhgüi*	ажиллахгүй
brothel	*yankhny ger*	янхны гэр
brown	*khüren*	хүрэн
brush	*soiz*	сойз
bucket	*khönög*	хөнөг
buckthorn	*chatsargan*	чацаргана
Buddha	*Burkhan*	Бурхан
Buddhist	*buddyn shashintan*	буддын шашинтан
building (house)	*baishing*	байшин
building (construction)	*barilag*	барилга
bulb (light)	*gerliin shil*	гэрлийн шил
bus	*avtobus*	автобус
bus station	*avtobusny buudal*	автобусны буудал
bus stop	*avtobusny zogsool*	автобусны зогсоол
business	*naimaa*	наймаа
businessperson	*naimaach*	наймаач
busy	*zavgüi*	завгүй
but	*kharin*	харин
button	*tovch*	товч
buy	*avakh*	авах

C

café	*tsainy gazar*	цайны газар
cairn (mound of stones)	*ovoo*	овоо
calculator	*tootsuur*	тооцуур
call (name)	*nerlekh*	нэрлэх

English	Romanized	Cyrillic
call (phone)	*utasdakh*	утасдах
call (shout)	*duudakh*	дуудах
camel	*temee*	тэмээ
camera	*zurag avuur*	зураг авуур
camp	*lager*	лагерь
can (able to)	*chadakh*	чадах
cannot	*chadakhgüi*	чадахгүй
can (preserve)	*konservyn laaz*	консервын лааз
can-opener	*laaz ongoiluur*	лааз онгойлуур
cancel	*khüchingüi bolgokh*	хүчингүй болгох
candle	*laa*	лаа
car (motor)	*suudlyn mashin/ tereg*	суудлын машин/ тэрэг
car (train)	*vagon*	вагон
card (name)	*neriin khuudas*	нэрийн хуудас
careful	*bolgoomjtoi*	болгоомжтой
carpet	*khivs*	хивс
carry	*bairj yavakh*	барьж явах
cart	*tereg*	тэрэг
case	*chemdan*	чемодан
cash (n)	*belen möng*	бэлэн мөнгө
cashier's	*kass*	касс
cassette	*khuurtsag/kasset*	хуурцаг/кассет
cassette player	*khuurtsag togluulagch*	хуурцаг тоглуулагч
Catholic	*katolik*	католик
cave	*agui*	агуй
CD	*kompakt disk*	компакт диск
cemetery	*orshuulgyn gazar*	оршуулгын газар
centre	*töv*	төв
century	*zuun (zuun jil)*	зуун (зуун жил)
certain (some)	*zarim*	зарим

VOCABULARY

certain (specific)	*todorkhoi*	тодорхой
certain (sure)	*zaaval*	заавал
chair	*sandal*	сандал
change (balance)	*khariult möng*	хариулт мөнгө
change (exchange)	*solikh*	солих
change (small)	*zadgai möng*	задгай мөнгө
cheap	*khyamd*	хямд
check (bill)	*tootsoo*	тооцоо
Cheers!	*erüül mendiin tölöö!*	Эрүүл мэндийн төлөө!
chemist's	*emiin sang*	эмийн сан
cheque	*chek*	чек
chequebook	*chekiin devter*	чекийн дэвтэр
chess	*shatar*	шатар
chewing gum	*boikh*	бохь
children	*khüükhed*	хүүхэд
china	*shaazang*	шаазан
China	*Khyatad Uls*	Хятад Улс
Chinese	*khyatad*	хятад
choose (elect)	*songokh*	сонгох
choose (select)	*songoj avakh*	сонгож авах
chopsticks	*savkh*	савх
Christian	*khristosyn shashintan*	христосын шашинтан
Christmas	*Khristosyn mendelsen ödör*	Христосын мэндэлсэн өдөр
church	*khristosyn süm*	христосын сүм
cigarette	*yanjuur*	янжуур
cinecamera	*kino avuur*	кино авуур
cinema	*kinoteatr*	кинотеатр
city	*khot*	хот
clean	*tseverkhen*	цэвэрхэн

VOCABULARY

clever	*sergeleng*	сэргэлэн
clock (watch)	*tsag*	цаг
closed (shop, etc)	*khaalttai*	хаалттай
clothes	*khuvtsas*	хувцас
a change of clothes	*khuvtsasny khalaa*	хувцасны халаа
cloud	*üül*	үүл
club	*klub*	клуб
coach (bus)	*ayany avtobus*	аяны автобус
coach (rail)	*vagon*	вагон
coffee	*kofi*	кофе
cold (temperature)	*khüiten*	хүйтэн
cold (head)	*nusgai*	нусгай
colour	*öng*	өнгө
come	*irekh*	ирэх
Come here!	*naash ir*	Нааш ир!
comfortable	*ayatai*	аятай
company (business)	*kompani*	компани
compartment	*öröö*	өрөө
complicated	*khetsüü*	хэцүү
computer	*tsakhim tootsooluur/*	цахим тооцоолуур/
	kompyuter	компьютер
concert	*kontsert*	концерт
condom	*belgevch*	бэлгэвч
conductor (bus)	*möng khuraagch*	мөнгө хураагч
conductor (music)	*khögjmiin*	хөгжмийн
	udirdaach	удирдаач
Congratulations!	*bayar hürgii!*	Баяр хүргэе!
consulate	*konsulyn gazar*	консулын газар
contagious	*khaldvartai*	халдвартай
contract (n)	*geree*	гэрээ
conversation	*yaria*	яриа
cook (n)	*togooch*	тогооч

cook (v)	*khool khiikh*	хоол хийх
cool	*serüün*	сэрүүн
copper	*zes*	зэс
cork	*böglöö*	бөглөө
cork screw	*böglöö sugaluur*	бөглөө сугалуур
corner	*bulang*	булан
correct	*zöv*	зөв
cost	*ün*	үнэ
costume (national)	*ardyn khuvtsas*	ардын хувцас
cot	*khüükhdiin or*	хүүхдийн ор
cotton (cloth)	*daavuu*	даавуу
cotton (wool)	*khövön*	хөвөн
cough	*khaniad*	ханиад
count	*toolokh*	тоолох
country (nation)	*uls*	улс
country (rural)	*khödöö nutag*	хэдээ нутаг
court	*shüükh*	шүүх
crazy	*soliotoi*	солиотой
credit card	*zeeliin/kredit kart*	зээлийн/кредит карт
cup	*ayag*	аяга
curtain	*khöshig*	хөшиг
customs (excise)	*gaail*	гааль
customs post	*boomt*	боомт
customs (habits)	*yos zanshil*	ёс заншил
cut (v)	*ogtlokh*	огтлох
cut off (v) (telephone)	*tasalchikhsan*	тасалчихсан

D

| dad/father | *aav/etseg* | аав/эцэг |
| daily | *ödör bür* | өдөр бүр |

damp	*noiton*	нойтон
dance	*büjig*	бүжиг
dangerous	*ayuultai*	аюултай
dark	*kharankhui*	харанхуй
date/day	*ödör*	өдөр
date (meet)	*uulzakh*	уулзах
dawn	*üür*	үүр
day/date	*ödör*	өдөр
dead	*nas barsan*	нас барсан
deaf	*dülii*	дүлий
debit card	*tölböriin kart*	төлбөрийн карт
decide	*shiidekh*	шийдэх
declaration	*gaaliin*	гаалийн
(customs)	*todorkhoilolt*	тодорхойлолт
deep	*gün*	гүн
delay	*saatuulakh*	саатуулах
delicious	*amttai*	амттай
delirious	*demüirsen*	дэмийрсэн
deliver	*damjuulakh*	дамжуулах
democracy	*ardchilal*	ардчилал
demonstration	*jagsaal*	жагсаал
dentist	*shüdnii emch*	шүдний эмч
deny	*ügüisgekh*	үгүйсгэх
depart	*yavakh*	явах
department store	*ikh delgüür*	их дэлгүүр
deposit (advance)	*uirdchilgaa*	урьдчилгаа
deposit (bank)	*khadgalamj*	хадгаламж
desert	*tsöl*	цөл
destroy	*süitgekh*	сүйтгэх
develop (something)	*bolovsruulakh*	боловсруулах
develop (film)	*todruulakh*	тодруулах
diaper/nappy	*chivkh*	чивх

dictionary	*toil bichig*	толь бичиг
different	*öör*	өөр
difficult	*khetsüü*	хэцүү
dining car	*khoolny vagon*	хоолны вагон
dining room	*khoolny öröö*	хоолны өрөө
dinner	*oroin khool*	оройн хоол
dinosaur	*üleg gürvel*	үлэг гүрвэл
diplomat/diplomatic	*diplomat*	дипломат
direction	*züg chig*	зүг чиг
dirty	*bokhir*	бохир
disabled	*gemtsen*	гэмтсэн
disco	*disko*	диско
discount	*khyamdruulakh*	хямдруулах
district (rural)	*sum*	сум
district (urban)	*düüreg*	дүүрэг
disturb	*üimüülekh*	үймүүлэх
divorced	*salsan*	салсан
dizzy	*tolgoi ergemeer*	толгой эргэмээр
Do it!	*khii!*	Хий!
Don't do it!	*bitgii!*	Битгий!
doctor	*emch*	эмч
doll	*naadgai*	наадгай
dollar	*dollar*	доллар
door/gate	*khaalag*	хаалга
dormitory	*niitiin bair*	нийтийн байр
double bed	*khoyor khünii or*	хоёр хүний ор
double room	*khoyor khünii öröö*	хоёр хүний өрөө
double (twin-bed) room	*khoyor ortoi öröö*	хоёр ортой өрөө
downstairs	*dood davkhart*	доод давхарт
downtown	*khotyn töv*	хотын төв
downwards	*dooshoo*	доошоо

dream	*züüd*	зүүд
dress	*platye*	платье
drink (n)	*undaa*	ундаа
drink (v)	*uukh*	уух
I'd like a drink.	*bi undaasch bain*	Би ундааси байна.
drinking water	*uukh us*	уух ус
drive (livestock)	*mal tuukh*	мал туух
drive (steer)	*joloodokh*	жолоодох
drive (vehicle)	*unaagaar yavakh*	унаагаар явах
driver	*jolooch*	жолооч
drug (medicine)	*em*	эм
drug (narcotic)	*mansuuruulakh bodis*	мансууруулах бодис
drunk (adj)	*sogtuu*	согтуу
dry/dried	*khuurai*	хуурай
dummy (baby's)	*khökhölt*	хөхөлт
dung (animal)	*argal*	аргал
duplicator	*khuviluur*	хувилуур
during	*... khugatsaand*	... хугацаанд
dust	*toos*	тоос
dustbin	*khogiin sav*	хогийн сав
duty (customs)	*tatvar*	татвар
duty (obligation)	*üüreg*	үүрэг

VOCABULARY

E

each	*neg bür*	нэг бүр
early	*ert*	эрт
earnings	*tsalin khöls*	цалин хөлс
earrings	*eemeg*	ээмэг
earthquake	*gazar khödlöl*	газар хөдлөл
east	*züün*	зүүн

Easter	*ulaan öndgiin bayar*	улаан өндөгийн баяр
easy	*amarkhan*	амархан
eat	*idekh*	идэх
economy (national)	*ediin zasag*	эдийн засаг
economy (saving)	*arvilakh*	арвилах
education	*bolovsrol*	боловсрол
either	*ail neg*	аль нэг
election	*songuuil*	сонгууль
electric/electricity	*tsakhilgaan*	цахилгаан
electric fan	*salkhin sens*	салхин сэнс
elevator	*lift*	лифт
embassy	*elchin yaam*	элчин яам
embroidery	*khatgamal*	хатгамал
emergency	*ayuultai baidal*	аюултай байдал
empty	*khooson*	хоосон
engineer	*injener*	инженер
English	*angil*	англи
enough	*khangalttai*	хангалттай
entertainment	*üzver*	үзвэр
entrance	*orts/orokh khaalag*	орц/орох хаалга
envelope (n)	*dugtui*	дугтуй
equal	*adil*	адил
especially	*yalanguyaa*	ялангуяа
evening	*üdesh*	үдэш
event	*üil yavdal*	үйл явдал
every	*... bür*	... бүр
excess baggage	*ilüü teesh*	илүү тээш
exchange	*solikh*	солих
exchange rate	*möngnii khansh*	мөнгөний ханш
Excuse me!	*uuchlaarai!*	Уучлаарай!
exhibition	*üzesgeleng*	үзэсгэлэн

VOCABULARY

exit	*garts/garakh*	гарц/гарах
	khaalag	хаалга
expensive	*üntei*	үнэтэй
experience	*turshlag*	туршлага
explain	*tailbarlakh*	тайлбарлах
explosive (n)	*tesremtgii bodis*	тэсрэмтгий бодис
export	*eksport*	экспорт
express (letter)	*yaaraltai zakhia*	яаралтай захиа
express (train)	*khurdan galt tereg*	хурдан галт тэрэг
extension cord	*dotuur utas*	дотуур утас

F

factory	*üildver*	үйлдвэр
faint (v)	*ukhaan balartakh*	ухаан балартах
fall (autumn)	*namar*	намар
fall (v)	*unakh*	унах
family	*ger bül*	гэр бүл
fan (electric)	*salkhiny sens*	салхины сэнс
far	*khol*	хол
fare	*unaany zardal*	унааны зардал
farmer (private)	*ardyn aj akhuitan*	ардын аж ахуйтан
fast (quick)	*khurdan*	хурдан
fast (not eat)	*matsag barikh*	мацаг барих
fat (grease)	*tos*	тос
fat (people)	*tarag*	тарга
fat (thick)	*zuzaan*	зузаан
faucet	*usny tsorog*	усны цорго
fault	*buruu*	буруу
It's my fault.	*minii buruu*	Миний буруу.
fax	*faks*	факс
fee	*khuraamj*	хураамж
feeding bottle	*ugj*	угж

VOCABULARY

felt (n)	*esgii*	эсгий
female (n)	*emegtei khün*	эмэгтэй хүн
ferry	*gatalag ongots*	гаталга онгоц
fever	*khaluun*	халуун
few	*tsöön*	цөөн
field/plain	*kheer tal*	хээр тал
fill (out — form)	*khuudas böglökh*	хуудас бөглөх
fill (pour)	*düürgekh*	дүүргэх
film (camera)	*khails*	хальс
film (cinema)	*kino*	кино
find	*olokh*	олох
fine (penalty)	*torguuil*	торгууль
fine (weather)	*saikhan*	сайхан
fire	*gal*	гал
fire extinguisher	*gal untraaguul*	гал унтраагуул
first	*ankhny*	анхны
first aid kit	*ankhny tuslamjiin kheregsel*	анхны тусламжийн хэрэгсэл
first-class (adj)	*negdügeer/ tergüün zergiin*	нэгдүгээр/ тэргүүн зэргийн
fishing rod	*zagasny uurag*	загасны уурга
flag (n)	*tug*	туг
flash (camera)	*gyalbuur*	гялбуур
flashlight	*gar chüdeng*	гар чийдэн
flat (appartment)	*oron suutsny bair*	орон сууцны байр
flat (level)	*khavtgai*	хавтгай
flight	*nisleg*	нислэг
flood	*üyer*	үер
flour	*guril*	гурил
flower	*tsetseg*	цэцэг

fly (v)	*nisekh*	нисэх
fog	*manang*	манан
folkmusic	*ardyn khögjim*	ардын хөгжим
follow	*dagakh*	дагах
food	*khool*	хоол
football	*khölbömbög*	хөлбөмбөг
ford (v)	*gatlakh*	гатлах
foreign	*gadaad*	гадаад
forget	*martakh*	мартах
Don't forget!	*bitgii martaarai!*	Битгий мартаарай
I/You forgot.	*bi/ta martjee.*	Би/Та мартжээ
forgive	*uuchlakh*	уучлах
fork	*seree*	сэрээ
form (class)	*ang*	анги
form (shape)	*khelber*	хэлбэр
forwards	*uragshaa*	урагшаа
free (cost)	*khölsgüi*	хөлсгүй
free (time)	*chölöötei*	чөлөөтэй
free (vacant)	*khüngüi*	хүнгүй
fresh	*shin*	шинэ
freeze	*khöldökh*	хөлдөх
friend	*naiz*	найз
friendly	*nökhörsög*	нөхөрсөг
frighten	*ailgakh*	айлгах
frost	*tsang*	цан
full	*düüreng*	дүүрэн
funny	*khögtei*	хөгтэй
furniture	*tavilag*	тавилга

G

game	*togloom*	тоглоом
garage (car)	*mashiny graj*	машины граж
garbage	*khog*	хог
garden	*tsetserleg*	цэцэрлэг
geology	*geologi*	геологи
gentleman	*eregtei*	эрэгтэй
gift	*beleg*	бэлэг
girl	*okhin*	охин
give	*ögökh*	өгөх
Give me ...	*nadad ... ögnüü?*	Надад ... өгнө уу?
glass (tumbler)	*shilen ayag*	шилэн аяга
glasses (spectacles)	*nüdnii shil*	нүдний шил
gloves	*beelii*	бээлий
glue	*tsavuu*	цавуу
go (away)	*yavakh*	явах
go (in)	*orokh*	орох
go (out)	*garakh*	гарах
goat	*yamaa*	ямаа
Gobi	*goiv*	говь
gold	*alt*	алт
good	*sain*	сайн
goodbye	*bayartai*	баяртай
goods	*baraa*	бараа
government	*zasgiin gazar*	засгийн газар
gram	*gramm*	грамм
grass/hay	*övs*	өвс
greasy	*tostoi*	тостой
grocer's	*khünsnii delgüür*	хүнсний дэлгүүр
guide (n)	*gazarch*	газарч
guidebook	*ayallyn lavlakh bichig*	аяллын лавлах бичиг

gun (hunting)	*(angiin) buu*	(ангийн) буу
gymnastics	*gimnastik*	гимнастик

H

hair	*üs*	үс
hairbrush	*üsnii soiz*	үсний сойз
hairdresser	*üschin*	үсчин
half	*khagas*	хагас
handbag	*gar tsünkh*	гар цүнх
handkerchief	*nusny alchuur*	нусны алчуур
handmade	*gar khiitsiin*	гар хийцийн
handsome	*saikhan*	сайхан
happy	*bayartai*	баяртай
hard (difficult)	*khetsüü*	хэцүү
hard (not soft)	*khatuu*	хатуу
hat	*malgai*	малгай
hate (dislike)	*... durgüi*	... дургүй
have		
I have ...	*nadad ... bain*	Надад ... байна.
You have...	*tand ... bain*	Танд ... байна.
Have you (got) ...?	*tand ... bainuu?*	Танд ... байна уу?
haven't (got)	*baikhgüi*	байхгүй
he	*ter (eregtei)*	тэр (эрэгтэй)
health	*erüül mend*	эрүүл мэнд
hear	*sonsokh*	сонсох
heating	*khalaalt*	халаалт
heavy	*khünd*	хүнд
helicopter	*nisdeg tereg*	Нисдэг тэрэг
Hello!	*sain bainuu!*	Сайн байна уу!
help	*tuslamj*	тусламж
herd	*süreg*	сүрэг
herding	*mal aj akhui*	мал аж ахуй

VOCABULARY

herdsman	*malchin*	малчин
here	*end*	энд
her	*tüünii (ter emegtein)*	түүний (тэр эмэгтэйн)
high	*öndör*	өндөр
hike (walk)	*yavgan ayalakh*	явган аялах
hill	*dov*	дов
hire	*khölslökh*	хөлслөх
We'd like to hire it.	*bid khölslön avmaar bain*	Бид хөлслөн авмаар байна
his	*tüünii (ter eregtein)*	түүний (тэр эрэгтэйн)
history	*tüükh*	түүх
hitchhike	*zamyn unaand daigdakh*	замын унаанд дайгдах
hobby	*sonirkhol*	сонирхол
holiday	*amralt*	амралт
home/felt tent (yurt)	*ger*	гэр
homesick (be)	*nutgaa sanakh*	нутгаа санах
honest	*shudrag*	шударга
honey	*bal*	бал
hope/trust (v)	*naidakh*	найдах
horse	*moir*	морь
horse racing	*moir uraldakh*	морь уралдах
hospital	*emneleg*	эмнэлэг
hot	*khaluun*	халуун
hot water/bathhouse	*khaluun us*	халуун ус
hotel	*zochid buudal*	зочид буудал
hour/clock	*tsag*	цаг
house/building	*baishing*	байшин
How far is it?	*ail kher khol ve?*	Алъ хэр хол вэ?

How many?	*kheden?*	Хэдэн?
How much?	*yamar üntei?*	Ямар үнэтэй?
How much is it?	*en yamar üntei ve?*	Эн ямар үнэтэй вэ?
How much do you need?	*khed kheregtei ve?*	Хэд хэрэгтэй вэ?
How is it done?	*yaaj khiikh?*	Яаж хийх?
How old are you?	*ta kheden nastai ve?*	Та хэдэн настай вэ?
hungry (be)	*ölsökh*	өлсөх
I'm hungry.	*bi ölsch bain*	Би өлсч байна.
hurry (be in a)	*yaarakh*	яарах
hurt (harm)	*gemteekh*	гэмтээх
hurt (pain)	*övdökh*	өвдөх
husband	*nökhör*	нөхөр

I

I	*bi*	би
ice	*mös*	мөс
idea	*sanaa*	санаа
idiot/idiotic	*teneg*	тэнэг
ill	*övchtei*	өвчтэй
illegal	*khuuil bus*	хууль бус
immediately	*darui*	даруй
import	*import*	импорт
important	*chukhal*	чухал
impossible (no chance)	*bolomjgüi*	боломжгүй
impossible (forbidden)	*bolokhgüi*	болохгүй
include	*bagtaakh*	багтаах
inconvenient	*ayagüi*	аягүй
incorrect	*buruu*	буруу

VOCABULARY

increase	*ösökh*	өсөх
individual (person)	*khün*	хүн
individual (private)	*khuviin*	хувийн
industry	*aj üildver*	аж үйлдвэр
inflation	*inflyatsi*	инфляци
informal	*chölööt*	чөлөөт
information office	*lavlakh tovchoo*	лавлах товчоо
insurance	*daatgal*	даатгал
intelligent	*ukhaantai*	ухаантай
interesting	*sonirkholtoi*	сонирхолтой
international	*olon ulsyn*	олон улсын
interpreter	*khelmerch*	хэлмэрч
introduce (people)	*taniltsuulakh*	танилцуулах
invalid (n)	*takhir dutuu khün*	тахир дутуу хүн
investment	*khöröng oruulalt*	хөрөнгө оруулалт
invitation	*urilag*	урилга
iron (metal)	*tömör*	төмөр
iron (press)	*indüü*	индүү
is/are/am	*bain*	байна
island	*aral*	арал
it	*ter (yum)*	тэр (юм)
its	*tüünii (ter yumny)*	түүний (тэр юмны)
itch	*zagatnaa*	загатнаа

J

jacket	*pidjak*	пиджак
jail	*shorong*	шорон
jam	*chanamal*	чанамал
jazz	*jazz*	джаз
jeans	*jeans*	жинс
jewellery	*alt möngön edlel*	алт мөнгөн эдлэл
job	*ajil*	ажил

VOCABULARY

joke	*shog*	шог
juice	*shüüs*	шүүс
jump	*kharaikh*	харайх

K

key	*tülkhüür*	түлхүүр
khan (king)	*khaan*	хаан
kill (people)	*alakh*	алах
kill (animals)	*nyadlakh*	нядлах
kilo	*kilogramm*	килограмм
kilometre	*kilometr*	километр
kind (sort)	*töröl*	төрөл
kind (person)	*sain setgeltei*	сайн сэтгэлтэй
kindergarten	*khüükhdiin tsetserleg*	хүүхдийн цэцэрлэг
kiss	*ünsekh*	үнсэх
kitchen	*gal zuukhny öröö*	гал зуухны өрөө
kite (paper)	*tsaasan shuvuu*	цаасан шувуу
knife	*khutag*	хутга
know (person)	*tanikh*	таних
know (thing)	*medekh*	мэдэх
koumiss	*airag*	айраг

L

label	*khayag*	хаяг
lace (shoe)	*uyaa*	уяа
lake	*nuur*	нуур
lama (monk)	*lam*	лам
lamp	*gerel*	гэрэл
land (plane)	*buukh*	буух
land (soil)	*gazar*	газар

landscape	*gazar nutgiin baidal*	газар нутгийн байдал
landslide	*khörsnii nuralt*	хөрсний нуралт
language	*khel*	хэл
large	*tom*	том
lasso	*uurag*	уурга
last	*süüliin*	сүүлийн
laugh (v)	*ineekh*	инээх
laundry (place)	*ugaalgyn gazar*	угаалгын газар
law	*khuuil*	хууль
laxative	*tuulag*	туулга
lazy	*zalkhuu*	залхуу
leader	*udirdagch*	удирдагч
learn	*surakh*	сурах
I'm learning ...	*bi ... surch bain*	Би ... сурч байна.
leather	*savikh*	савхи
leave (go away)	*yavakh*	явах
leave (go out)	*garakh*	гарах
leave (holiday)	*amralt*	амралт
left (side)	*züün*	зүүн
legal	*khuuiltai*	хуультай
lend	*tür ögökh*	түр өгөх
lens (magnifying)	*galt shil*	галт шил
lens (camera)	*durang*	дуран
less	*bag khemjee*	бага хэмжээ
letter	*zakhidal*	захидал
letter writing paper	*zakhidal bichikh tsaas*	захидал бичих цаас
liar	*khudalch*	худалч
library	*nomyn sang*	номын сан
lid	*tag*	таг
life	*aimdral*	амьдрал

lift (elevator)	*lift*	лифт
lift (give)	*zamdaa dairch avakh*	замдаа дайрч авах
lift (raise)	*örgökh*	өргөх
light (lamp)	*gerel*	гэрэл
light (weight)	*khöngön*	хөнгөн
lighter (n)	*asaaguur*	асаагуур
lightning	*tsakhilgaan*	цахилгаан
like	*durtai*	дуртай
I like ...	*bi ... durtai*	Би ... дуртай.
I don't like ...	*bi ... durgüi*	Би ... дургүй.
Do you like ...?	*ta ... durtai yuu?*	Та ... дуртай юу?
lip	*uruul*	уруул
listen	*sonsokh*	сонсох
litre	*litr*	литр
little	*jijig*	жижиг
live (reside)	*suukh*	суух
livestock	*aduu mal*	адуу мал
long	*urt*	урт
long-distance call	*kholyn duudlag*	холын дуудлага
look (appear)	*kharagdakh*	харагдах
look (see)	*kharakh*	харах
lorry	*achaany mashin*	ачааны машин
lose	*khayakh*	хаях
lost property	*khayasan yum*	хаясан юм
love	*khairtai*	хайртай
I love you.	*bi chamd khairtai*	Би чамд хайртай.
low	*nam*	нам
luck	*az*	аз
luggage	*achaa*	ачаа
lunch	*üdiin khool*	үдийн хоол

M

English	Romanization	Cyrillic
machine/vehicle	*mashin*	машин
mad (be angry)	*uurlakh*	уурлах
mad (wild)	*galzuu*	галзуу
magazine	*setgüül*	сэтгүүл
mail (post)	*shuudang*	шуудан
main	*gol*	гол
make	*khiikh*	хийх
male	*eregtei khün*	эрэгтэй хүн
man	*khün*	хүн
manager	*erkhlegch*	эрхлэгч
many	*olon*	олон
map	*gazryn zurag*	газрын зураг
mare	*güü*	гүү
market	*zakh*	зах
married	*gerlesen*	гэрлэсэн
massage	*illeg*	иллэг
matches	*shüdenz*	шүдэнз
maybe	*magadgüi*	магадгүй
meal	*khool*	хоол
measure (on a scale)	*khemjikh*	хэмжих
measure (step taken)	*arag khemjee*	арга хэмжээ
mechanic	*mekhanik*	механик
medicine	*em*	эм
meet	*uulzakh*	уулзах
We'll meet you.	*bid tautai uulzan*	Бид тантай уулзан.
mend (clothes)	*nökhökh*	нөхөх
message	*zakhia*	захиа
metal	*metall*	металл
method	*arag*	арга
metre	*metr*	метр

middle (in the)	*dundad*	дундад
mineral water	*rashaan us*	рашаан ус
minute (time)	*minut*	минут
minute (tiny)	*mash jijig*	маш жижиг
mirror	*toil*	толь
miss (long for)	*sanakh*	санах
miss (target)	*onokhgüi*	онохгүй
mist	*budang*	будан
mistake	*aldaa*	алдаа
modern	*orchin üyiin*	орчин үеийн
monastery	*khiid*	хийд
money	*möng*	мөнгө
Mongolia	*Mongol Uls*	Монгол Улс
Mongolian	*mongol*	монгол
month/moon	*sar*	сар
monument	*khöshöö*	хөшөө
more	*dakhiad*	дахиад
motor	*khödölgüür*	хөдөлгүүр
motorcycle	*mototsikl*	мотоцикл
mountain	*uul*	уул
mouth	*am*	ам
move	*khödlökh*	хөдлөх
movie	*kino*	кино
mud	*shavar*	шавар
museum	*muzei*	музей
music	*khögjim*	хөгжим
musical instrument	*khögjmiin zemseg*	хөгжмийн зэмсэг
Muslim (n)	*lalyn shashintan*	лалын шашинтан
must (obliged)	*yostoi*	ёстой
must (needed)	*kheregtei*	хэрэгтэй
my	*minii*	миний

N

nail (wood)	*khadaas*	хадаас
name (n)	*ner*	нэр
nappy/diaper	*chivkh*	чивх
national (country)	*ulsyn*	улсын
national (people)	*ündesnii*	үндэсний
natural	*baigaliin*	байгалийн
nature	*baigail*	байгаль
near	... *oir*	... ойр
needed	*kheregtei*	хэрэгтэй
needle (sewing)	*züü*	зүү
needle (hypo)	*tariany züü*	тарианы зүү
negative	*negativ*	негатив
new	*shin*	шинэ
news	*medee*	мэдээ
newspaper	*sonin*	сонин
next	*daraa*	дараа
next of kin	*oiryn töröl*	ойрын төрөл
nice	*saikhan*	сайхан
night	*shön*	шөнө
No. (not at all)	*ügüi*	Үгүй.
No. (not this)	*bish*	Биш.
noisy	*shuugiantai*	шуугиантай
nomad	*nüüdelchin*	нүүдэлчин
normal	*kheviin*	хэвийн
north	*khoid*	хойд
now	*odoo*	одоо
number	*dugaar*	дугаар

O

obvious	*todorkhoi*	тодорхой
occupation	*mergejil*	мэргэжил

police	*tsagdaa*	цагдаа
police station	*tsagdaagiin gazar*	цагдаагийн газар
politics	*uls tör*	улс төр
pool (swimming)	*bassein*	бассейн
poor (poverty)	*yaduu*	ядуу
poor (quality)	*muu*	муу
post (n)	*shuudang*	шуудан
post (v)	*shuudangaar yavuulakh*	шуудангаар явуулах
post box	*shuudangiin khairtsag*	шуудангийн хайрцаг
post office	*shuudangiin salbar*	шуудангийн салбар
pottery	*vaaran edlel*	вааран эдлэл
preferable	*ilüü*	илүү
prepare	*beltgekh*	бэлтгэх
present (gift)	*beleg*	бэлэг
president	*yörönkhiilögch*	ерөнхийлөгч
pressure	*daralt*	даралт
pretty	*saikhan*	сайхан
price	*ün*	үнэ
prison	*shorong*	шорон
private	*khuviin*	хувийн
probably	*bolzoshgüi*	болзошгүй
problem	*asuudal*	асуудал
product	*büteegdekhüün*	бүтээгдэхүүн
profession	*mergejil*	мэргэжил
programme (plan)	*khötölbör*	хөтөлбөр
programme (theatre)	*program*	программ
promise	*amlakh*	амлах
pronunciation	*duudlag*	дуудлага
property	*ömch*	өмч

office	*alban gazar*	албан газар
officer (mil)	*ofitser*	офицер
official (adj)	*alban*	албан
official (n)	*alban khaagch*	албан хаагч
often	*olon udaa*	олон удаа
oil (petroleum)	*gazryn tos*	газрын тос
OK	*zügeer*	зүгээр
old (people)	*nastai*	настай
old (things)	*khuuchin*	хуучин
on	*... deer*	... дээр
only	*zövkhön*	зөвхөн
open (shop, etc)	*ongorkhoi*	онгорхой
operator (tel)	*zalgagch*	залгагч
opinion	*sanal*	санал
opportunity	*saikhan bolomj*	сайхан боломж
opposite/anti-	*... esreg*	... эсрэг
or	*buyuu*	буюу
order (food)	*zakhialakh*	захиалах
ordinary	*engiin*	энгийн
organisation	*baiguullag*	байгууллага
other	*öör*	өөр
our	*manai*	манай
outside	*gadan*	гадна
overnight (v)	*khonokh*	хонох
owe	*örtei baikh*	өртэй байх
I/You owe ...	*bi/ta ... örtei*	Би/Та ... өртэй.

P

packet	*baglaa*	баглаа
page	*khuudas*	хуудас
painting	*uran zurag*	уран зураг

VOCABULARY

pair	*khos*	хос
palace	*ordon*	ордон
paper	*tsaas*	цаас
parcel	*ilgeemj*	илгээмж
park (car)	*bairlakh gazar*	байрлах газар
park (garden)	*tsetserleg*	цэцэрлэг
party (political)	*nam*	нам
party (social)	*tsaillag*	цайллага
pass (mountain)	*davaa*	даваа
passenger	*zorchigch*	зорчигч
passport (internal ID)	*irgenii pasport*	иргэний паспорт
passport (foreign travel)	*gadaad pasport*	гадаад паспорт
path/road	*zam*	зам
pay	*tölökh*	төлөх
peace	*enkh taivan*	энх тайван
pedestrian	*yavgan khün*	явган хүн
pen (animals')	*khashaa*	хашаа
pen (ink)	*üzeg*	үзэг
pensioner	*tetgever avagch*	тэтгэвэр авагч
people	*khümüüs*	хүмүүс
percentage	*zuuny khuiv*	зууны хувь
performance/show	*shii jüjig*	ший жүжиг
perfume	*sürchig*	сүрчиг
perhaps	*magadgüi*	магадгүй
period (menses)	*saryn temdeg*	сарын тэмдэг
period (time)	*khugatsaa*	хугацаа
permit (v)	*zövshöörökh*	зөвшөөрөх
person	*khuiv khün*	хувь хүн
personal	*khuviin*	хувийн
petrol	*benzin*	бензин

VOCABULARY

perspire	khöls tsutgakh	хөлс цутгах
pharmacy	emiin sang	эмийн сан
photocopier	olshruulagch	олшруулагч
photocopy (n)	kseroks	ксерокс
photograph	gerel zurag	гэрэл зураг
Can I take photos?	bi zurag avch bolokhuu?	Би зураг авч болох уу?
Can I take your photograph?	bi tany zurgiig avch bolokhuu?	Би таны зургийг авч болох уу?
photographer	zuragchin	зурагчин
phrasebook	yariany devter	ярианы дэвтэр
picnic	ayany zuush	аяны зууш
piece	kheseg	хэсэг
pill	ürel	үрэл
pilot	nisegch	нисэгч
pin/needle	züü	зүү
pin (hair)	khatguur	хатгуур
pin (safety)	sülbeer züü	сүлбээр зүү
pipe (tobacco)	gaans	гаанс
pipe (water)	khooloi	хоолой
place	gazar	газар
plane	nisekh ongots	нисэх онгоц
plastic	khuvantsar	хуванцар
plate	tavag	таваг
platform	davtsan	давцан
play (n)	jüjig	жүжиг
play (v)	toglokh	тоглох
plug (basin)	böglöö	бөглөө
plug (electric)	zalguur	залгуур
pocket	khalaas	халаас
pocket knife	evkhdeg khutag	эвхдэг хутг
poisonous	khortoi	хортой

prostitute	*yankhan*	янхан
protect	*khamgaalakh*	хамгаалах
province	*aimag*	аймаг
public (adj)	*olon niitiin*	олон нийтийн
pull	*tatakh*	татах
purse/wallet	*khetevch*	хэтэвч
push	*tülkhekh*	түлхэх
put	*tavikh*	тавих

Q

quality	*chanar*	чанар
quantity	*too khemjee*	тоо хэмжээ
quarrel	*kherüül*	хэрүүл
quarter (fourth)	*dörvönii neg*	дөрөвний нэг
quarter (town)	*düüreg*	дүүрэг
queen	*khatan khaan*	хатан хаан
question	*asuult*	асуулт
queue (v)	*daraalald zogsokh*	дараалалд зогсох
quick	*khurdan*	хурдан
quiet	*taivan*	тайван

R

radio	*raju*	радио
railway	*tömör zam*	төмөр зам
railway carriage	*galt tergenii vagon*	галт тэрэгний вагон
railway station	*galt tergenii buudal*	галт тэрэгний буудал
rain	*boroo*	бороо
raincoat	*boroony tsuv*	борооны цув
rape (v)	*khüchindekh*	хүчиндэх

VOCABULARY

rare	*khovor*	ховор
raw	*tüükhii*	түүхий
razor	*khusuur*	хусуур
razor blade	*sakhlyn khutag*	сахлын хутга
read	*unshikh*	унших
ready	*belen*	бэлэн
real	*bodit*	бодит
really	*ünendee*	үнэндээ
reason	*uchir*	учир
receipt	*tasalbar*	тасалбар
receiver (radio)	*khüleen avagch*	хүлээн авагч
recent	*önöö üyiin*	өнөө үеийн
receptionist	*zochid khüleen avagch*	зочид хүлээн авагч
recommend (advise)	*zövlökh*	зөвлөх
record (disk)	*pyanz*	пянз
record (sound)	*bichikh*	бичих
record (sport)	*deed amjilt*	дээд амжилт
record (written)	*protokol*	протокол
record player	*togluulagch*	тоглуулагч
refrigerator	*khörgögch*	хөргөгч
registered (letter)	*batalgaatai*	баталгаатай
relationship	*kholboo*	холбоо
relatives	*khamaatan*	хамаатан
religion	*shashin*	шашин
remember	*sanakh*	санах
rent (hire)	*khölslökh*	хөлслөх
repair	*zasvarlakh*	засварлах
repeat		

Repeat that please.   *ta terniig dakhiad kheleed ögööch*   Та тэрнийг дахиад хэлээд өгөөч.

report (v)	*iltgekh*	илтгэх
representative	*tölöölögch*	төлөөлөгч
reptile	*khevleer yavagch*	хэвлээр явагч
reserve (v)	*uirdchilan zakhialakh*	урьдчилан захиалах
responsibility	*khariutslag*	хариуцлага
rest (v)	*amrakh*	амрах
restaurant	*zoogoi*	зоогой
return (come back)	*butsaj irekh*	буцаж ирэх
return (give back)	*ögökh*	өгөх
return (go back)	*butsaj yavakh*	буцаж явах
revolution	*khuivsgal*	хувьсгал
rich	*bayan*	баян
right (correct)	*zöv*	зөв
right (hand)	*baruun*	баруун
ring	*bögj*	бөгж
ripe	*belen*	бэлэн
river	*gol/mörön*	гол/мөрөн
road/path	*zam*	зам
rock (cliff)	*khad*	хад
rock (stone)	*chuluu*	чулуу
roof	*deever*	дээвэр
room	*öröö/tasalgaa*	өрөө/тасалгаа
room number	*öröönii dugaar*	өрөөний дугаар
rubbish	*khog*	хог
rucksack	*üürgevch*	үүргэвч
ruined (in ruins)	*evderkhii*	эвдэрхий
run (v)	*güikh*	гүйх

S

sad	*gunigt*	гунигт
saddle	*emeel*	эмээл
safe (adj; secure)	*ayuulgüi*	аюулгүй
safe (n; lockup)	*seif*	сейф
salt	*davs*	давс
same	*adil*	адил
sand	*els*	элс
sandals	*sandaal*	сандаал
sand dunes	*mankhan els*	манхан элс
satisfactory	*khangalttai*	хангалттай
say	*khelekh*	хэлэх
scenery (nature)	*baigail*	байгаль
school	*surguuil*	сургууль
scissors	*khaich*	хайч
screwdriver	*khaliv*	халив
sculpture	*barimal*	баримал
second (2nd)	*khoyordugaar*	хоёрдугаар
second (of time)	*sekund*	секунд
second-class (adj)	*khoyordugaar zergiin*	хоёрдугаар зэргийн
secret	*nuuts*	нууц
secretary (title)	*nariin bichgiin darag*	нарийн бичгийн дарга
secretary (clerk)	*bicheech*	бичээч
see	*üzekh*	үзэх
self	*ööröö*	өөрөө
self-service	*öörtöö üilchildeg*	өөртөө үйлчилдэг
sell	*khudaldakh*	худалдах
send	*ilgeekh*	илгээх
sentence (words)	*ögüülbör*	өгүүлбөр
sentence (court)	*niitleg*	нийтлэг

serious	*chukhal*	чухал
service (rendered)	*üilchilgee*	үйлчилгээ
sew	*oyokh*	оёх
sex (act)	*khuirtsal*	хурьцал
sex (gender)	*khüis*	хүйс
shape	*khelber*	хэлбэр
shave	*sakhal khusakh*	сахал хусах
shaver	*britv*	бритв
shaving soap	*sakhlyn savang*	сахлын саван
she	*ter (emegtei)*	тэр (эмэгтэй)
sheet (bed)	*orny tsagaan daavuu*	орны цагаан даавуу
sheet (paper)	*khuudas*	хуудас
ship	*usan ongots*	усан онгоц
shop	*delgüür*	дэлгүүр
short	*bogin*	богино
shower	*shürshüür*	шүршүүр
shut (shop, etc)	*khaalttai*	хаалттай
shy	*ichimtgii*	ичимтгий
sick (unwell)	*övchtei*	өвчтэй
sick (to vomit)	*bööljikh*	бөөлжих
side	*tal*	тал
sightseeing	*dursgalt gazruudyg üzekh*	дурсгалт газруудыг үзэх
signature	*garyn üseg*	гарын үсэг
silver	*möngön*	мөнгөн
simple	*engiin*	энгийн
since	*...khoish*	... хойш
sing	*duulakh*	дуулах
single (alone)	*gants*	ганц
single (unmarried)	*gerleegüi`*	гэрлээгүй
single room	*neg khünii öröö*	нэг хүний өрөө

sit	*suukh*	суух
situation	*baidal*	байдал
size (clothes)	*razmer*	размер
size (scale)	*khemjee*	хэмжээ
sky/weather	*tenger*	тэнгэр
sleep (v)	*untakh*	унтах
sleeping bag	**uu**tan *khönjil*	уутан хөнжил
sleeping car	*untlagyn vagon*	унтлагын вагон
sleepy	*noirmog*	нойрмог
slide (photo)	*diapozitiv*	диапозитив
slow	*udaan*	удаан
small (size)	*jijig*	жижиг
small change	*zadgai möng*	задгай мөнгө
smelly	*ömkhii*	өмхий
smile (v)	*ineekh*	инээх
smoke	*tatakh*	татах
snow	*tsas*	цас
soap	*savang*	саван
soccer	*khölbömbög*	хөлбөмбөг
sock/stocking	*oims*	оймс
soft	*zöölön*	зөөлөн
soil (v)	*buzarlakh*	бузарлах
soil (n)	*khörs*	хөрс
some	*zarim*	зарим
sometimes	*zarimdaa*	заримдаа
song	*duu*	дуу
soon	**u**dakhgüi	удахгүй
Sorry!	*uuchlaarai!*	Уучлаарай!
south	*ömön*	өмнө
souvenir	*beleg dursgal*	бэлэг дурсгал
spa	*arshaang*	рашаан
speak	**ya**rikh	ярих

special	*ontsgoi*	онцгой
speed	*hurd*	хурд
sport	*sport*	спорт
spring (season)	*khavar*	хавар
spring (water)	*bulag*	булаг
square (place)	*talbai*	талбай
square (rectangle)	*dörvöljin*	дөрвөлжин
stadium	*tsengeldekh khüreelen*	цэнгэлдэх хүрээлэн
stairs	*shat*	шат
stall/small shop	*mukhlag*	мухлаг
stamp (rubber)	*tamag*	тамга
stapler	*üdüür*	үдүүр
star	*od*	од
state	*uls*	улс
station	*buudal*	буудал
stationery	*bichgiin kheregsel*	бичгийн хэрэгсэл
statistics	*too bürtgel*	тоо бүртгэл
stay (remain)	*üldekh*	үлдэх
stay (visit)	*ochikh*	очих
stick (n)	*mod*	мод
stick (v)	*naakh*	наах
stirrup	*döröö*	дөрөө
stop	*zogsokh*	зогсох
Stop!	*zogs!*	Зогс!
store (shop)	*delgüür*	дэлгүүр
storey	*davkhar*	давхар
storm	*shuurag*	шуурга
story	*tuuj*	тууж
stove	*zuukh*	зуух
straight ahead	*chigeeree*	чигээрээ
street	*gudamj*	гудамж
string/thread/wire	*utas*	утас

student	*oyuutan*	оюутан
study	*surakh*	сурах
stupid	*teneg*	тэнэг
strange	*khachin*	хачин
stranger (n)	*gadny khün*	гадны хүн
stupa	*suvrag*	суврага
success	*amjilt*	амжилт
suit (n)	*kostyum*	костюм
suit (v)	*taarakh*	таарах
suitcase	*chemdan*	чемодан
summer	*zun*	зун
sun	*nar*	нар
sunburn (catch)	*narand sharakh*	наранд шарах
sunglasses	*narny shil*	нарны шил
suntan cream	*narny tos*	нарны тос
supermarket	*khünsnii ikh delgüür*	хүнсний их дэлгүүр
swim	*usand selekh*	усанд сэлэх
swimming pool	*bassein*	бассейн
swimsuit	*usny khuvtsas*	усны хувцас
switch (light)	*untraalag*	унтраалга
syringe (needle)	*tariany züü*	тарианы зүү
system	*juram*	журам

T

table	*shiree*	ширээ
table tennis	*shireenii tennis*	ширээний теннис
tailor	*oyodolchin*	оёдолчин
take	*avakh*	авах
talk	*yarikh*	ярих
tall	*öndör*	өндөр

VOCABULARY

tap	*usny tsorog*	усны цорго
tape (recording)	*khails*	хальс
tape recorder	*magnitofon*	магнитофон
tasty	*amttai*	амттай
tax	*tatvar*	татвар
taxi	*taksi*	такси
teacher	*bagsh*	багш
team	*bag*	баг
telegram	*tsakhilgaan*	цахилгаан
telephone	*utas*	утас
telephone directory	*utasny jagsaalt*	утасны жагсаалт
telephone number	*utasny dugaar*	утасны дугаар
telephoto lens	*tatakh durang*	татах дуран
television	*televiz/zuragt*	телевиз/зурагт
television set	*televizor*	телевизор
telex	*teleks*	телекс
tell	*khelekh*	хэлэх
temple	*süm*	сум
tent (felt)	*ger*	гэр
tent (summer)	*maikhan*	майхан
thank	*bayarlakh*	баярлах
Thank you!	*tand bayarlaa!*	Танд баярлалаа!
that	*ter*	тэр
theatre	*teatr*	театр
their	*tednii*	тэдний
then (at that time)	*ter üyed*	тэр уед
then (next)	*daraa*	дараа
there	*tend*	тэнд
thermos	*khaluun sav*	халуун сав
they	*ted*	тэд
theft	*khulgai*	хулгай
thick	*zuzaan*	зузаан

VOCABULARY

thief	*khulgaich*	хулгайч
thin	*nimgen*	нимгэн
thing	*yum*	юм
think	*bodokh*	бодох
thirst (v)	*am tsangaj bain*	ам цангаж байна
I'm thirsty.	*minii am tsangaj bain*	Минийн ам цангаж байна.
this	*en*	энэ
thread/string/wire	*utas*	утас
throw	*khayakh*	хаях
throw away	*gargaj khayakh*	гаргаж хаях
thunder	*tengeriin duu*	тэнгэрийн дуу
ticket	*bilet/tasalbar*	билет/тасалбар
tight (clothes)	*bariu*	бариу
time/clock	*tsag*	цаг
timetable	*tsagiin khuvaair*	цагийн хувaарь
tin	*konservyn laaz*	консервын лааз
tin-opener	*laaz ongoiluur*	лааз онгойлуур
tip (cash)	*shang/garyn möng*	шан/гарын мөнгө
tired	*tsutssan*	цуцсан
We are tired.	*bid yadarsan*	Бид ядарсан.
tissues	*tsaasan alchuur*	цаасан алчуур
tobacco	*tamikh*	тамхи
today	*önöödör*	өнөөдөр
together	*khamt*	хамт
toilet	*jorlong*	жорлон
Where is the toilet?	*jorlong khaan baidag ve?*	Жорлон хаана байдаг вэ?
toilet paper	*jorlongiin tsaas*	жорлонгийн цаас
tomorrow	*margaash*	маргааш
tonight	*önöö oroi*	өнөө орой
too (also)	*bas*	бас

too (much)	*dendüü*	дэндүү
top	*oroi*	орой
torch	*gar chiideng*	гар чийдэн
tortoise	*yast melkhii*	яст мэлхий
tour (n)	*ayalal*	аялал
tourist	*juulchin*	жуулчин
towards	*... ruu*	... руу
towel	*nüür garyn alchuur*	нүүр гарын алчуур
town	*khot*	хот
toy	*togloom*	тоглоом
tractor	*traktor*	трактор
trade	*khudaldaa*	худалдаа
trade union	*üildverchnii evlel*	үйлдвэрчний эвлэл
tradition	*ulamjlal*	уламжлал
traffic (road)	*zamyn khödölgöön*	замын хөдөлгөөн
traffic lights	*gerel dokhio*	гэрэл дохио
train	*galt tereg*	галт тэрэг
transfer (send)	*damjuulakh*	дамжуулах
transit	*tranzit*	транзит
translate	*orchuulakh*	орчуулах
translator	*orchuulagch*	орчуулагч
travel (move)	*khödlökh*	хөдлөх
travel (tour)	*ayalakh*	аялах
travel agency	*juulchdad üilchlekh tovchoo*	жуулчдад үйлчлэх товчоо
travellers' cheque	*juulchny chek*	жуулчны чек
tree/wood	*mod*	мод
truck (lorry)	*achaany mashin*	ачааны машин
trust (v)	*itgekh*	итгэх
try (attempt)	*oroldokh*	оролдох
try (court)	*shüükh*	шүүх
try (on)	*ömsch üzekh*	өмсч үзэх

tugrik	*tögrög*	төгрөг
turn (direction)	*ergelt*	эргэлт
turn (opportunity)	*eelj*	ээлж
twice	*khoyor udaa*	хоёр удаа
typewriter	*bichgiin mashin*	бичгийн машин

U

ugly	*muukhai*	муухай
uncomfortable	*tukhgüi*	тухгүй
under	*door*	доор
understand	*oilgokh*	ойлгох
I understand.	*bi oilgoj bain*	Би ойлгож байна.
I don't understand.	*bi oilgokhgüi bain*	Би ойлгохгүй байна.
unemployed	*ajilgüi*	ажилгүй
United Nations	*Negdsen Ündestnii Baiguullag*	Нэгдсэн Үндэстний Байгууллага
university	*ikh surguuil*	их сургууль
unsatisfactory	*khangaltgüi*	хангалтгүй
until	*... khürtel*	... хүртэл
upstairs	*deed davkhart*	дээд давхарт
upwards	*deeshee*	дээшээ
urgent	*yaaraltai*	яаралтай
use (v)	*khereglekh*	хэрэглэх
useful	*kheregtseetei*	хэрэгцээтэй

V

vacancy	*sul oron too*	сул орон тоо
vacuum flask	*khaluun sav*	халуун сав
validity (duration)	*khugatsaa*	хугацаа
valley	*khöndii*	хөндий

VOCABULARY

valuable	*ikh üntei*	их үнэтэй
very	*mash*	маш
vessel (pot)	*sav*	сав
vessel (ship)	*ongots*	онгоц
veteran	*akhmad*	ахмад
videocamera	*videokamer*	видеокамер
videocassette	*videokasset*	видеокассет
videorecorder	*videomagnitofon*	видеомагнитофон
village	*tosgon*	тосгон
visa	*viz*	виз
visit	*ochikh*	очих
visitor	*zochin*	зочин
voice	*duu*	дуу
vomit (v)	*bööljikh*	бөөлжих
vote	*songokh*	сонгох
vulgar	*soyolgüi*	соёлгүй

W

wage	*tsaling*	цалин
waist	*belkhüüs*	бэлхүүс
wait	*khüleekh*	хүлээх
waiter/waitress	*üilchlegch*	үйлчлэгч
waiting room	*khüleelgiin öröö*	хүлээлгийн өрөө
wake (someone)	*sereekh*	сэрээх
walk	*yavgan yavakh*	явган явах
wall	*khan*	хана
wallet/purse	*khetevch*	хэтэвч
want (wish)	*khüsekh*	хүсэх
want (need)	*kheregtei*	хэрэгтэй
I/We want ...	*nad/bidend ...*	Над/Бидэна ...
	kheregtei	хэрэгтэй.

VOCABULARY

VOCABULARY

war	*dain*	дайн
warm	*dulaan*	дулаан
wash	*ugaakh*	угаах
washing powder	*ugaalgyn nuntag*	угаалгын нунтаг
water	*us*	ус
waterfall	*khürkhree*	хүрхрээ
way (method)	*arag*	арга
way (road/path)	*zam*	зам
Which way to ...?	*... yaaj yavakh ve?*	... Яаж явахж вэ?
we	*bid*	бид
weak (health)	*sul biitei*	сул биетэй
wear (put on clothes)	*ömsökh*	өмсөх
weather	*tenger/tsag uur*	тэнгэр/цаг уур
wedding	*khurim*	хурим
week	*doloo khonog*	долоо хоног
well	*khudag*	худаг
west	*baruun*	баруун
wet	*noiton*	нойтон
What?	*yuu?*	Юу?
What is this?	*en yuu ve?*	Энэ юу вэ?
What kind of?	*yamar?*	Ямар?
What kind of room have you got?	*yamar öröötei yum be?*	Ямар өрөөтэй юм бэ?
wheat	*buudai*	буудай
When?	*khezee?*	Хэзээ?
When will you come?	*ta khezee irekh ve?*	Та хэзээ ирэх вэ?
Where?	*khaan?*	Хаана?
Where are you going?	*ta khaashaa yavj bain ve?*	Та хаашаа явж байиа вэ?

Where is the toilet?	*jorlong khaan baidag ve?*	Жорлон хаана байдаг вэ?
Which?	*yamar?*	Ямар?
Who?	*khen?*	Хэн?
wide	*örgön*	өргөн
wildlife	*zerleg aimtad*	зэрлэг амьтад
win (game)	*khonjikh*	хонжих
win (war)	*yalakh*	ялах
wind (n)	*salikh*	салхи
window	*tsonkh*	цонх
wine	*dars*	дарс
wire/thread/string	*utas*	утас
withdraw (take out)	*butsaaj avakh*	буцааж авах
without	*... -güi*	... -гүй
woman	*emegtei*	эмэгтэй
wood (forest)	*oi*	ой
wood (wooden)	*mod*	мод
wool	*noos*	ноос
word	*üg*	үг
work	*ajil*	ажил
world	*delkhii*	дэлхий
worst	*khamgiin muu*	хамгийн муу
wound	*sharkh*	шарх
wrestling	*bökh*	бөх
write	*bichikh*	бичих
writing paper	*bichgiin tsaas*	бичгийн цаас
wrong	*buruu*	буруу

X

x-ray (plate)	*rentgen zurag*	рентген зураг

VOCABULARY

Y

yak	*sarlag*	сарлаг
year	*on/jil*	он/жил
yes	*tiim*	тийм
yesterday	*öchigdör*	өчигдөр
you (child, close friend)	*chi*	чи
you (polite form)	*ta*	та
young (people)	*zaluu*	залуу
young (animals)	*töl*	төл
your (child, close friend)	*chinii*	чиний
your (polite form)	*tany*	таны
youth hostel	*zaluuchuudyn bair*	залуучуудын байр
yurt (felt tent)	*ger*	гэр

Z

zero	*teg*	тэг
zip	*tsakhilgaan tovch*	цахилгаан товч
zone	*büs*	бүс
zoo	*aimtny khüreelen*	амьтны хүрээлэн

Emergencies

Help!	*tuslaarai!*	Туслаарай!
Police!	*tsagdaa!*	Цагдаа!
Thief!	*khulgaich!*	Хулгайч!
Fire!	*gal!*	Гал!
Stop!	*zogs!*	Зогс!
Watch out!	*kharaa!*	Хараа!
Go away!	*zail!*	Зайл!

Please don't do that!
bitgii tegeerei!
Битгий тэгээрэй!

Don't do it again!
dakhiad büü teg!
Дахиад бүү тэг!

I've been robbed!
namaig deeremdlee!
Намайг дээрэмдлээ!

They took my ...	*ted minii ... avsan*	Тэд миний ... авсан.
backpack	*üürgevchiig*	үүргэвчийг
bag	*uutyg*	уутыг
camera	*zurag avuuryg*	зураг авуурыг
money	*möngiig*	мөнгийг
passport	*pasportyg*	паспортыг
purse/wallet	*khetevchiig*	хэтэвчийг
wristwatch	*buguin tsagiig*	бугуйн цагийг

Where are the toilets?
jorlon khaan bain ve?
Жорлон хаана байна вэ?

Where is the police station?
  tsagdaagiin gazar khaan bain ve?

Цагдаагийн газар хаана байна вэ?

Can you show me?
  ta nadad üzüülenüü?

Та надад үзүүлнэ үү?

Please write it down.
  ta nadad bichij ögööch!

Та надад бичиж өгөөч!

There's been an accident!
  osol garchee!

Осол гарчээ!

Call a doctor!
  emch duudaarai!

Эмч дуудаарай!

Call an ambulance!
  türgen tuslamj duudaarai!

Түргэн тусламж дуудаарай!

Call the police!
  tsagdaa duudaarai!

Цагдаа дуудаарай!

I've been raped.
  namaig khüchindlee

Намайг хүчиндлээ

I am ill.
  bi övchtei bain

Би өвчтэй байна.

Please take me to hospital.
  namaig emnelegt khürgej ögnüü

Намайг эмнэлэгт хүргэж өгнө үү?

My blood group is (A, B, O, AB) positive (negative).
  minii tsusny büleg (Ah, Bay, Oh, AhBay) nemekh (khasakh)

Миний цусны бүлэг (А, Б, О, АБ) нэмэх (хасах).

next of kin
  oiryn töröl

ойрын төрөл

Show me your I.D.
ta ünemlekhee üzüülenüü?   Та үнэмлэхээ үзүүлнэ үү?

I don't understand.
bi oilgokhgüi bain   Би ойлгохгүй байна.

Does anyone speak English?
*angilar yardag khün
bainuu?*   Англиар ярьдаг хүн байна уу?

Could you help me please?
ta nadad neg tus bolooch?   Та надад нэг тус болооч?

I've lost my way.
bi zamaasaa töörchikhlöö   Би замаасаа төөрчихлөө?

I'm sorry.
uuchlaarai!   Уучлаарай!

Please forgive me!
ta namaig uuchlaarai!   Та намайг уучлаарай!

I didn't realise I was doing
something wrong.
*bi sanaandgüi muukhai
yum khiilee*   Би санаандгүй муухай
юм хийлээ.

I didn't do anything.
bi yaagaachgüi   Би яагаа ч үгүй.

I didn't do it.
bi yuch khiigeegüi   Би юу ч хийгээгүй.

Please could I use your
phone?
tany utsaar yairj bolokhuu?   Таны утсаар ярьж болох уу?

I wish to contact my embassy.
*bi elchin yaamtaigaa
yarimaar bain*   Би элчин яамтайгаа
яримаар байна.

Index

Sustainable Travel

As the climate change debate heats up, the matter of sustainability becomes an important part of the travel vernacular. In practical terms, this means assessing our impact on the environment and local cultures and economies – and acting to make that impact as positive as possible. Here are some basic phrases to get you on your way …

Communication & Cultural Differences

I'd like to learn some of your local dialects.

bi tanai nutgiin ayalgyg surmaar baina   Би танай нутгийн аялгыг сурмаар байна.

Would you like me to teach you some English?

ta jaakhan angli khel zaalgamaar bainuu?   Та жаахан англи хэл заалгамаар байна уу?

Is this a local or national custom?

ene tanai undesnii zan zanshiluu?   Энэ танай үндэсний зан заншил уу?

I respect your customs.

bi tanai zan zanshlyg khundetgej baina   Би танай зан заншлыг хүндэтгэж байна.

Community Benefit & Involvement

What sorts of issues is this community facing?

ene nutgiinkhand yamar asuudal tulgarch baina ve?   Энэ нутгийнханд ямар асуудал тулгарч байна вэ?

205

alcoholism	*arkhidalt*	архидалт
indigenous	*nutgiin irgediin*	нутгийн иргэдийн
rights	*erkh zörchigdökh*	эрх зөрчигдөх
poverty	*yaduural*	ядуурал

I'd like to volunteer my skills.
bi chadvaraa ashiglan   Би чадвараа ашиглан
sain duryn ajild   сайн дурын ажилд
oroltsmoor baina   оролцмоор байна.

Are there any volunteer programs available in the area?
ene nutagt sain duryn   Энэ нутагт сайн дурын
khötölbör bii yüü?   хөтөлбөр бий юу?

Environment

Does your company have a green policy?
tanai kompanid baigali   Танай компанид байгаль
orchny bodlogo bii yüü?   орчны бодлого бий юу?

Where can I recycle this?
bi üüniig khaana khayakh ve?   Би үүнийг хаана хаях вэ?

Transport

Can we get there by public transport?
bid tiishee niitiin   Бид тийшээ нийтийн
teevreer ochij bolokhuu?   тээврээр очиж болох уу?

Can we get there by bike?
bid tiishee unadag   Бид тийшээ унадаг
duguigaar ochij   дугуйгаар очиж
bolokhuu?   болох уу?

I'd prefer to walk there.
bi tiishee alkhmaar baina   Би тийшээ алхмаар байна.

Accommodation

I'd like to stay at a locally-run hotel.

bi oron nutgiin
buudald buumaar baina

Би орон нутгийн
буудалд буумаар байна.

Are there any ecolodges here?

end ekobuudal bii yüü?

Энд эко-буудал бий юү?

Can I turn the air conditioning off and open the window?

bi agaarjuulagchiig untraaj,
tsonkhoo neej bolokhuu?

Би агааржуулагчийг унтрааж,
цонхоо нээж болох уу?

There's no need to change my sheets.

minii daavuug solikh
khereggui

Миний даавууг солих
хэрэггүй.

Shopping

Where can I buy locally produced souvenirs?

nutgiin irgediin khiisen
beleg dursgalyn zuiliig
khaanaas khudaldan
avch bolokh ve?

Нутгийн иргэдийн хийсэн
бэлэг дурсгалын зүйлийг
хаанаас худалдан
авч болох вэ?

Is this made
from ...?

üüniig ...
khiisen üü?

Үүнийг ...
хийсэн үү?

antlers	*bugyn evreer*	бугын эврээр
saxaul root	*zagiin ündseer*	загийн үндсээр
snow leopard skin	*irvesiin arisaar*	ирвэсийн арьсаар

Food

Do you sell locally produced food?

tanaid nutgiin khünsnii
büteegdkhüün zardaguu?

Танайд нутгийн хүнсний
бүтээгдхүүн зардаг уу?

Do you sell organic produce?
tanaid organik khünsnii
büteegdkhüün zardaguu?
Танайд органик хүнсний
бүтээгдхүүн зардаг уу?

Can you tell me which traditional foods I should try?
ulamjlalt yamar yamar
khünsnii büteegdkhüünees
idej üzvel zügeer ve?
Уламжлалт ямар ямар
хүнсний бүтээгдхүүнээс
идэж үзвэл зүгээр вэ?

Sightseeing

Does your company donate money to charity?
tanai kompani buyany
baiguullagad khandiv
örgödög üü?
Танай компани буяны
байгууллагад хандив
өргөдөг үү?

Does your company hire local guides?
tanai kompani nutgiin
irgediig hötchöör
ajilluuldaguu?
Танай компани нутгийн
иргэдийг хөтчөөр
ажиллуулдаг уу?

Does your company visit local businesses?
tanai kompani oron
nutgiin aj akhuin
negjüüdtei khariltsdaguu?
Танай компани орон
нутгийн аж ахуйн
нэгжүүдтэй харилцдаг уу?

Are cultural tours available?
tanaikh soyolyn ayalal
zokhiodoguu?
Танайх соёлын аялал
зохиодог уу?

Does the guide speak …?	*khötöch … kheleer yaridaguu?*	Хөтөч … хэлээр ярьдаг уу?
Kazakh	*kazakh*	казах
Tuvan	*tuva*	тува

SIGNS

ОРЦ	**Entrance**
ГАРЦ	**Exit**
ОРЖ БОЛОХГҮЙ	**\No Entrance**
ГАРЧ БОЛОХГҮЙ	**No Exit**
ЭМЭГТЭЙН	**Ladies**
ЭРЭГТЭЙН	**Gentlemen**
ТАТ	**Pull**
ТУЛХ	**Push**
ХАДГАЛСАН	**Reserved/Engaged**
ХООСОН	**Vacant**
ЕРӨНХИЙ ЖИЖҮҮР	**Reception**
КАСС	**Cashier**
ЛАВЛАГАА	**Information**
ШУУДАН	**Post**
ТАКСИ	**Taxi**
ХААСАН	**Closed**
СУУДАЛГҮЙ	**Sold Out**
БОЛГООМЖИЛ	**Caution**
ЗАСВАРТАЙ	**Under Repair**
ТАМХИ ТАТАЖ БОЛОХГҮЙ	**No Smoking**
ЗУРАГ АВЧ БОЛОХГҮЙ	**No Photography**